COOKING FOR MENIERE'S THE LOW SALT WAY

ITALIAN

PAGE ADDIE PRESS
UNITED KINGDOM AUSTRALIA

Copyright

Contents

MENIERE MAN UNSALTED

Wars were fought for salt. Roads were built to transport salt. Taxes were levied in salt; people smuggled salt; Roman soldiers were paid in salt and if someone did not work properly, he was not "worth his salt".

Before refrigeration, salt was used to cure and preserve meat and fish so they could be eaten all year round. Today, most of the salt we consume comes, not from adding salt to fresh foods, but from processed foods. We often eat salt unconsciously. Foods like salami, hard cheese, olives, bacon, ham and anchovies for starters. Every gram of hidden salt adds up.

Food you eat out, tastes different to the food you cook at home. There's a reason for this. Chefs in a restaurant kitchen, use a lot of salt. If you could see behind the scenes of red and white checked table cloths and smiling waiters: you would see handfuls of salt going into every pot of pasta, into sauces, over meat, onto fish and into vegetables. Enough salt to give you vertigo.

You won't find any added salt or processed foods in our Italian recipes. You will find recipes for no salt mozzarella, ricotta, pizza, lasagna and even a famous recipe for a deli style sweet Italian sausage, all full of flavor, instead of full of salt.

Before I was diagnosed with Meniere's, my favorite foods started with the letter S for salt: Saga blue cheese, salami, sausage, sauerkraut, soy sauce, spare ribs, string cheese and Swedish fish (especially the one in a jar with caper mayonnaise) and sea salt. Yes, I was a heavy salt user.

Meniere's meant I had to quit salt and change the habit of a lifetime. However, maintaining a sodium intake below 1000mg a day took some effort. So how much salt do we need? A normal salt diet is 1100-3300mg a day. A recommended healthy low salt diet for Menieres is 400 - 1000mg a day. The body needs some salt; you can't live without salt.

Salt enough for your daily needs, is found in natural whole foods, such as meat, fish, fruit, nuts, grains and vegetables. There's *absalt- lutely* no need to add a grind of sodium chloride, in other words: rock salt, table salt, smoked salt, seasoned salt, iodized salt, sea salt, black salt, lava salt, truffle salt, bamboo salt, garlic salt, celery salt, pickling salt, or add a shake of pink salt, that has been carried in sacks, on the backs' of yaks, 260 kilometres down from the Himalayas. When you have Meniere's, the last thing you need in the world is salt!

COOKING THE LOW SALT WAY

I wrote this new cookbook for everyone who has been diagnosed with Meniere's and been told to cut out salt by their doctor. And then wondered... what can I eat? How can I enjoy my favorite foods, like pizza and pastas, without salt?

This book is about the love of food and not about counting salt grams. I initially counted grams but it was such a frustrating, and anxious activity, I stopped. Recent studies have shown that strict salt regulation, fuels anxiety and may worsen symptoms. We don't count salt grams, but we don't add salt and we avoid hidden sodium in these recipes.

'Cooking For Meniere's The Low Salt Way', is not a diet. It's about changing the habit and quiet addiction to salt, but still eating the food you love...like Italian. I was lucky enough to go to Italy for a month. Many things struck me about the local food...seeing vine tomatoes ripening in the sun; a plate full of grilled anchovies, the sweet smell of fresh basil, sage green olive oil drizzled on garlic toasted bread; dusky purple figs for dessert. I love the clean flavors of Italian food, how the scent of lemon or fresh basil linger in the air while you cook. Food full of intensity, as if the land, sun, sea and history are intrinsic ingredients in every traditional Italian recipe.

The act of cooking low salt can be as simple and easy as your busy day has time for. I've learned all sorts of tricks along the way: like how to make my own pasta sauces for spaghetti and lasagna and how to make my own ricotta and mozzarella cheese without salt.

You can have masses of flavor without loads of salt. When you eat this way, your taste buds adapt quickly; a slice of fresh grain bread, eaten without salty butter, has a grainy taste instead of a salted buttery taste. I promise you this, by *Cooking the Low Salt Way*© you won't miss your salt shaker.

Food is about pleasure, which is the way it should be. I think the biggest benefit of a eating the low salt way is that we taste, smell and appreciate the flavors of our food more. This cookbook is for everyone who enjoys good food, friends, family, love and laughter. These are all powerful health boosters and exactly what you need when you have Meniere's. I hope you enjoy cooking and eating the low salt way as much as we do.

COOKING THE LOW SALT WAY

THE ITALIAN
PANTRY

No Salt Mozzarella Cheese

One slice of bought whole milk mozzarella can contain 178mg of sodium. One slice of bought low sodium mozzarella contains 5mg. Here is a recipe for homemade mozzarella which has no salt added. You can make this recipe in 30 minutes. Less than the time it takes to go to the supermarket to find the bought version.

Makes: about 500g
Cooking time: 30 minutes

Ingredients

4.5 liters of whole milk

1 1/2 tsp citric acid

1/4 tablet rennet

mineral water

* Do not use junket rennet for making mozzarella, as it is not strong enough.

Method

Mix citric acid in 1 cup cold water.

Pour milk into a heavy bottomed saucepan. Stir in citric acid mixture.

Heat the milk to 32 degrees C, stirring constantly. Remove from heat. Dissolve rennet tablet in 1/4 cup cool water. Add this slowly to the milk using an up and down motion with a slotted metal spoon. Cover with a lid. Let stand for 5 minutes. Remove lid and check the curd. It should resemble custard when pressed lightly with your finger.

Take a metal knife or spatula. Slice across the surface of the curd cutting the curd into 3cm squares. Return the saucepan to the heat and heat the curd to 40 degrees C, while slowly stirring the curd with your spoon. Remove from heat and stir for 2-5 minutes. The more you stir the firmer the mozzarella will be. Pour into a sieve or colander. The curds will drain off from the whey (the liquid). Pour curds into a microwavable bowl. Tip bowl to drain off whey. Microwave on high for 1 minute. Drain off the whey again. Microwave again for 30 seconds. Remove from bowl and place curds on a workbench. Knead, as you would bread dough, turning the cheese and folding the cheese over. Keep kneading until the cheese turns glossy. If cheese doesn't hold together, microwave for another 30 seconds on high.

Cheese is ready when it is so elastic that you can stretch into a long strand.

Form the cheese into a loaf shape or a ball. You can plait the cheese also. Then fill a bowl with cool water and submerge the cheese for 15 minutes. This will help the cheese keep its shape and maintain a silky texture.

Cheese keeps in the fridge in a covered container for up to 2 weeks. You can also wrap the cheese tightly in cling film and freeze it.

Hot water bath directions

If you don't have a microwave you can create mozzarella by using the following method. Follow cheese-making steps in the recipe up to the microwave instructions. Instead of using the microwave, heat water in a heavy saucepan to 82 degrees C. Spoon the curds into a colander or sieve, folding the curds over gently as you drain off the whey. Dip the colander into the hot water several times. Take a spoon and fold the curds until they become elastic and pliable. Remove the curds, stretch and pull. If it does not stretch easily, return to the hot water bath in the colander and repeat the process. Then continue kneading cheese until it is pliable like long elastic. Submerge in water for 15 minutes. Drain. Store covered in the fridge as directed.

No Salt
Ricotta Cheese

Homemade ricotta cheese is as cheap to make as the cost of a liter of milk. Homemade ricotta makes a great base for ravioli fillings and lasagna. You can serve with freshly sliced fruit: peaches, nectarines and berries. Or with stewed stone fruit: apricots, plums or fresh figs served with a drizzle of honey.

Makes: 2 cups
Cooking time: 30 minutes

Ingredients

8 cups whole milk
1 cup plain whole milk yogurt
1/2 cup heavy cream (optional for richer cheese)
2 tsp white wine vinegar or lemon juice

Method

Heat milk, yogurt and cream (if using) and vinegar in a heavy-bottomed saucepan.
Bring to boil on medium heat. Turn heat to low and boil very gently for 2 minutes, or until milk is curdled.

Remove from heat. Line a sieve or colander with 2 layers of clean cheesecloth or fine washed muslin. Set the colander into a deep bowl. Pour the milk mixture into the lined colander or sieve. Drain for 15 minutes. Pull sides of the cloth together and squeeze the curds gently to remove the whey (liquid). Remove strained curds from cloth and serve. You can store the ricotta cheese, in a covered container in the fridge for up to 3 days.

No Salt Mascarpone Cheese

This fresh curd cheese originated in the 16th century. This homemade version has a sweet buttery flavor. You can use it to make Italian desserts or simply serve with fresh fruit.

Ingredients

500 ml low fat cream (25%)
1 tbsp lemon juice

Method

Heat cream in an heatproof bowl over a saucepan filled with simmering water, until it reaches 80 degrees C. Stir in lemon juice until it starts to thicken. Remove from heat and cover and let sit at room temperature until cooled down. Refrigerate overnight. Pour the mixture into a sieve lined with 3 layers of cheesecloth or muslin. Place in fridge for 24 hours to let the whey drain.Remove cheese and store in a covered container in the fridge.

No Salt Chicken Stock

Ingredients

2 tbsp extra virgin olive oil

1 kg chicken carcass, bones and wings, washed

3 medium carrots, cut in chunks

2 brown onions, cut in chunks

4 stalks celery

5 stalks parsley

2 tsp whole black peppercorns

Method

Heat oil in a large heavy-bottomed saucepan.
Add chicken bones and brown. Take care not to
burn or stock will be bitter. Remove chicken bones.
Add onions, celery, carrots and cook until soft.
Add bones back into the saucepan. Add enough
cold water to cover the chicken bones. Add
peppercorns, cooked onion mixture and parsley.
Bring to boil and immediately reduce heat to low.
Simmer on low heat for 2 hours. Remove from heat.
Strain through a sieve or colander. Discard solids.

No Salt
Vegetable Stock

Ingredients

2 liters of water

2 medium brown onions

4 large carrots

4 stalks celery

8 cloves garlic

2 large tomatoes

1 potato

2 dried bay leaves, 2 sprigs fresh thyme

8 sprigs parsley, 5 black peppercorns

1 tbsp olive oil

Method

Wash vegetables and chop into 2 cm chunks.
Heat oil in a large saucepan. Add vegetables
and herbs. Cook on high heat for 5 minutes while
stirring. Add water to the pan. Bring to the boil then
reduce heat to simmer. Simmer uncovered for 30
minutes. Strain vegetables. Discard. Reserve the
stock. Cool and store in fridge. Stock freezes well.

Basil Pesto

Traditional pasta sauce from Genoa.

Makes: 1 cup

Ingredients

2 cups (packed) fresh basil leaves
1 clove garlic, peeled
1 tsp black pepper, freshly ground
Approximately 2/3 cup extra-virgin olive oil
1/2 cup pine nuts, lightly toasted in a frying pan

Method

Place basil leaves, pine nuts, garlic and pepper in a food processor until finely chopped. While the motor is running, slowly add the olive oil in a thin stream. Add just enough oil to make a smooth and thick sauce. Season with more pepper if needed. Store in a covered jar in the fridge. Use as a sauce over hot pasta.

Sugo di Pomodoro

This authentic recipe is the oldest and most famous tomato sauce in Italian cooking.

Serves: 6
Cooking time: 30 minutes

Ingredients

400g can crushed Italian no low salt tomatoes
3 cloves garlic
6 tbsp olive oil
1/2 tsp coarsely ground black pepper
1/2 tsp sugar
fresh basil, large bunch, chopped finely

Method

Peel garlic cloves and chop into medium to fine pieces. Heat olive oil in a heavy bottomed pan and add garlic. Sauté until golden, taking care not to brown. Add tomatoes. On high heat, bring to boil while stirring constantly. Lower heat to medium. Add pepper and sugar. Stir well.
Turn heat to low and simmer for 20 minutes until

thick stirring at regular intervals to prevent the
sauce from sticking to the pan.
Remove from heat, add basil.

S u g o
d i   P o m o d o r o
(B i g   f r e e z e r   b a t c h)

If fresh tomatoes are not plentiful, use no added salt tinned Italian Roma tomatoes. Freeze in batches so it is always available.

Makes: 2.5 liters
Cooking time: 2 hours

Ingredients

8 x 400g cans peeled Italian tomatoes, no salt

3 bay leaves

2 tsp dried oregano

2 tsp dried basil

200ml olive oil

6 large onions, chopped finely

5 cloves garlic, chopped finely

black pepper, freshly ground

Method

Place tomatoes in a large bowl and mash down with a potato masher. Add bay leaves, basil and oregano. Heat oil in a large sauce pan. Add onions and garlic and cook over low to medium heat taking care not to brown. About 5 minutes. Add tomato mixture. Reduce heat to low and simmer, stirring occasionally for 2 hours. Season with pepper. Cool. Place in containers in the freezer in measured portions for convenience. Use in pasta and pizza recipes.

Caramelized Onion Balsamic Jam

Serves: 4 - 6
Cooking time: 1 hour

Ingredients

2 tbsp olive oil

2 tbsp unsalted butter

4 cups Spanish red onions thinly sliced

1/4 cup water

2 tbsp balsamic vinegar

1 tbsp brown sugar

1 tbsp fresh thyme leaves, chopped

2 bay leaves

freshly ground black pepper

Method

Heat oil in a large saucepan over medium heat. Add onions. Stir. Cook over medium high heat, stirring occasionally until onions are soft, about 10 - 15 minutes. Add thyme and bay leaves. Reduce heat and cook over low for 3 minutes. Sprinkle sugar over onions. Cook without stirring until sugar caramelizes, about 5 minutes. Add balsamic vinegar and stir until jam thickens, about 5 minutes. Add freshly ground black pepper to taste.

Serve warm at room temperature on crusty bread or as an accompaniment to roast beef, rack of lamb, chicken, grilled salmon or ocean fish.

ANTIPASTI

Tomato Bruschetta

Grilled bread topped with fresh tomatoes and basil is a Tuscan favorite.

Serves: 4
Cooking time: 10 minutes

Ingredients

4 acid free ripe tomatoes, finely chopped
fresh basil leaves
ground black pepper
3 cloves garlic, peeled
crusty Italian bread, sliced approx 1 cm thick
extra virgin olive oil

Method

Place basil leaves, tomatoes, pepper and olive oil in a small bowl. Grill bread in an oven or charcoal flame. When both sides are golden, remove from heat. Immediately rub the garlic cloves over the toasted bread. Place bread on a serving plate and top with the tomato mixture.

Variation

To make mushroom bruschetta, heat a little olive oil with two cloves of garlic, some chopped parsley, a small sprig of fresh marjoram or 1/2 tsp fresh oregano leaves. Add 150g diced button mushrooms and 100g fresh brown mushrooms. When cooked place mushroom mixture on top of toasted bread and serve with a fresh basil leaf on top of each toast.

Crostini di Pepperoni

Roasted peppers on toasted bread.

Serves: 6
Cooking time: 30 minutes

Ingredients

1 large red bell pepper (capsicum)
1 large yellow bell pepper (capsicum)
4 cloves of garlic, peeled
fresh basil leaves, coarsely shredded
black pepper
extra virgin olive oil
crusty farmhouse style bread, sliced 1 cm thick

Method

Wash peppers and grill in the oven or over a gas
flame. The skins will blister and turn black in color.
Place chargrilled peppers inside a plastic. Seal
the bag and leave the peppers to sweat for 30
minutes. Remove the skin and deseed the peppers
but keep the juices. Cut peppers into thin strips.
Place in a bowl with the pepper juice, freshly

ground black pepper, olive oil to taste and basil leaves. Set aside for 10 minutes. Place on grilled bread and top with fresh basil leaves.

Stuffed Mushrooms

Serves: 6 - 8
Cooking time: 30 minutes

Ingredients

1/2 cup dried crumbs from Italian style bread

2 garlic cloves, minced

3 tbsp Italian parsley leaves, chopped

1 tbsp mint leaves, chopped

freshly ground black pepper

1/4 cup olive oil

20 large button mushrooms, stalks removed

Method

Heat oven to 190 degrees C.

Place breadcrumbs in a bowl. Add garlic, parsley, mint and pepper.

Grease a large baking dish with 1 tbsp olive oil. Place mushrooms top side down on the baking dish. Place a tsp of filling into each mushroom (where the stalk was). Drizzle a little oil over each mushroom. Bake in a hot oven until the filling is cooked, about 20 minutes and the top of each mushroom is golden. Serve as an appetizer, on toasted bread, or drizzle with a little balsamic and serve as a vegetable accompaniment for a main dish of roasted meat or chicken.

Purea di Fave

Fava bean puree can be used as a dip for vegetables, on toasted pita or toasted crostini.

Serves: 4 - 6
Cooking time: 2 hours

Ingredients

300g dried fava (broad) beans, soaked 12 hours
1 potato, peeled and diced
extra virgin olive oil
white or black pepper, freshly ground

Method

Soak beans overnight. Rinse and put them into a large saucepan. Add potato. Cover with water and bring to the boil. Turn heat down to simmer. Simmer beans for 2 hours. Skim froth as it rises to the surface. When beans are done, mash them to a puree or use a food processor for a smoother texture. Serve with a drizzle of olive oil on top.

Mescciua

Recovery soup

Ingredients

2 tbsp extra virgin olive oil

200g chickpeas

200g white beans

200g orzo pasta

1 small bunch flat-leaf Italian parsley

Method

Soak chickpeas and white beans in a bowl overnight. Drain the water from the beans and place beans in a saucepan. Cover with fresh water. Simmer on low heat for 1 hour until almost cooked. Place orzo in a saucepan. Add two cups water and 2 tbsp olive oil. Bring to the boil over medium heat. Reduce to simmer. Drain cooked beans and add to orzo. Cook 10 - 15 minutes until orzo is cooked. Serve in small bowls topped with a little olive oil, freshly ground pepper and chopped flat-leaf Italian parsley.

R i b o l i t a

Tuscan bean soup

Serves: 6 - 8
Cooking time: 1 hour

Ingredients

500g dried cannellini beans

400g dried borlotti beans

freshly ground black pepper

1 liter low salt vegetable or chicken stock

8 tbsp extra virgin olive oil

5 stalks celery, finely chopped

3 medium carrots, finely chopped

3 cloves garlic, crushed

3 bay leaves

1 sprig fresh rosemary

Italian flat-leaf parley leaves for garnish

Method

Soak beans, each in a separate bowl overnight.
Rinse well. Drain. Place beans in separate pans
with enough water to cover. Cook borlotti beans
for 1 hour. Cook cannellini beans for 45 minutes.

Drain and set aside. While beans are cooking, take a large frying pan. Make a 'soffritto': by cooking celery, garlic, onions, rosemary and bay leaves together on medium heat in the oil. Cook until the onions soften and the mixture is golden, taking care not to brown, or the onions will taste bitter. Season with black pepper. Remove the rosemary and bay leaves. Discard.

Place the vegetable stock and cannellini beans in a large saucepan. Add onion mixture. Bring to boil, reduce heat to medium low and simmer for 30 minutes, until beans become tender but not soft and mushy. Add borlotti beans. Heat through. Pour into serving bowls and drizzle with extra-virgin olive oil and garnish with Italian parsley leaves.

Serve with crusty bread.

Tuscan Bean & Barley Soup

Serves: 4 - 6
Cooking time: 30 minutes

Ingredients

2 cloves garlic, crushed

3 medium carrots, diced

3 celery stalks, diced

2 medium leeks, white part only, chopped

900 ml homemade chicken stock

2 tbsp tomato puree

4 tbsp pearl barley, rinsed and drained

400g borlotti beans, soaked overnight and cooked
1 hour, drain

200g fresh baby spinach leaves

olive oil

Method

Heat 2 tbsp olive oil in a large saucepan. Add
garlic, celery, carrots and leeks. Cook on medium
heat until vegetables are soft. Add chicken stock,

barley and tomato puree. Turn heat down low and simmer for 20 minutes until the barley is tender. Take care not to overcook the barley. You want it slightly firm and nutty. Add beans and spinach and cook for 5 minutes. Serve hot with fresh crusty bread and a grind of pepper.

Minestrone

More minestrone is eaten in Italy than pasta, making this vegetable soup, Italy's favorite.

Serves: 6 - 8
Cooking time: 40 minutes

Ingredients

6 cups of homemade, no salt beef stock.

4 carrots, cut in cubes

1 large onion, diced

2 stalks celery

100gms green beans

1 large zucchini, sliced thinly

5 cloves garlic, peeled and chopped

1/4 head of cabbage, chopped

2 cans of no salt Italian Roma tomatoes

1 can no salt cannellini beans

3 medium potatoes, peeled and diced

3 tbsp Italian parley, chopped

3 tbsp olive oil

250g Italian pasta

Method

In a large saucepan, sauté in oil, garlic, onions, carrots, green beans, potatoes, celery for 10 minutes, stirring to prevent the vegetables sticking to the pan. Add zucchini and cabbage. Cook for 5 minutes. Add tomatoes, parsley, basil and cannellini beans. Add beef stock and ground black pepper. Bring to boil over a medium heat. Turn heat down and simmer for about 20 minutes until vegetables are cooked. Cook pasta in another pan for 10 minutes. Drain. Place pasta in each soup bowl and add the vegetable soup. Sprinkle with shredded fresh basil leaves or chopped fresh parsley. Serve with crusty bread.

COOKING THE LOW SALT WAY

PASTA

Spaghetti Bolognese

The sofritto (flavor base) of celery, garlic, onions and carrots, gives this sauce a rich flavor.

Serves: 4 - 6
Cooking time: 40 minutes

Ingredients

2 tbsp olive oil

2 large onions

3 garlic cloves

2 carrots, peeled and chopped

1 stick celery, chopped

1 kg lean minced beef

2 large glasses red wine

2 x 400g cans no salt Italian chopped tomatoes

2 bay leaves

freshly ground black pepper

1 pinch sugar

500g fresh spaghetti or 400g dried pasta

Method

Heat oil in a heavy-based pan. Fry onions and
garlic until golden color but not brown. Take care
not to burn. Turn heat to high and add minced
beef. Fry until browned. Add wine and simmer on
low heat for 10 minutes. Add tomatoes, chopped
celery, carrots and a pinch of sugar. Cover and
simmer on low heat for 1 hour until the sauce is
rich and thick. Stir occasionally to prevent sauce
sticking to the pan. Serve over freshly cooked
pasta. Top with basil leaves and ground pepper.

Bolognese Ragu

The longer and slower the cooking, the more the flavors blend and concentrate, slowly reducing and thickening to make this a rich traditional Italian pasta sauce.

Serves: 6
Cooking time: 2 hours

Ingredients

500g fresh tagliatelle or 400g dried pasta

4 tbsp olive oil

1 large carrot, peeled and finely chopped

1 stalk celery, chopped

1 onion, finely chopped

150g minced beef

150g minced pork

chicken or beef stock, no salt added, or water

4 tbsp tomato paste

400g can no salt crushed Roma tomatoes

freshly ground black pepper

10 fresh basil leaves

Method

Heat oil in a heavy-bottomed pan over medium heat. Add onion, celery and carrots. Cook until golden brown. Add the meat. Cook for 10 minutes until the meat browns. Add wine and cook for a few minutes more. Add tomatoes and tomato paste diluted with a little stock or water. Stir. Simmer on low heat stirring occasionally for 90 minutes. Add more stock or water as ragu cooks. The finished ragu should be rich and smooth. Season with pepper. Cook pasta in boiling water until just soft but still firm (al dente). Drain in a colander and place on serving plates or in bowls. Add sauce and garnish with fresh basil leaves (optional).

This sauce can be used whenever you need a beef filling to make baked cannelloni or beef lasagna.

Cannelloni Ricotta Spinach

In Italian, cannelloni means 'large reeds'. Spinach and ricotta go together in this healthy version with nutmeg and black pepper.

Serves: 6 - 8
Cooking time: 40 minutes

For the tomato sauce

Ingredients

2 tbsp olive oil

1 small onion, finely chopped

2 cloves garlic, peeled and finely chopped

1 cup fresh basil, finely chopped

1/2 cup white wine

handful of fresh basil leaves

1 kg ripe tomatoes, coarsely chopped

freshly ground black pepper

Method

Heat oil in a large pan and add onions, garlic.
Sauté until golden. Add tomatoes, basil leaves and
1/2 cup water. Simmer for 30 minutes on low heat.
Cool. Then blend to a smooth paste. Set aside.

For the bechamel sauce

Ingredients

5 tbsp unsalted butter
4 tbsp plain flour
4 cups milk
1/2 tsp freshly grated nutmeg
pepper

Method

Heat milk slowly in a pan until just reaching the boil.
Meanwhile, melt butter in a medium saucepan
on low heat. Add flour mixing until smooth with a
wire whisk. Cook over low heat for 6 minutes until
light brown. Add hot milk whisking all the time until
smooth. Bring to the boil. Cook the sauce for 8
minutes, stirring to prevent sauce burning. Remove
from heat. Season with freshly grated pepper and
nutmeg. Set aside.

For the spinach filling

Ingredients

2 eggs

1 large bunch of fresh spinach leaves

(or use frozen spinach) cooked, drained, chopped

500g low salt ricotta or no salt cottage cheese

freshly ground black pepper

2 pinches of freshly grated nutmeg

18 dried cannelloni tubes

Method

Place all ingredients into a bowl. Mix well and season with pepper and nutmeg. Set aside.

To assemble the cannelloni, spoon ricotta spinach mixture into dried cannelloni tubes.

Place half the tomato sauce on the bottom of a greased rectangular or square (oven to table) baking dish. Place cannelloni tubes on top of the sauce. Next drizzle the bechamel sauce over the cannelloni. Add the rest of the tomato sauce. Drizzle with a little olive oil. Cover baking dish with foil. Bake in a 180 C degree oven for about 30 minutes. Remove foil and bake for 5 - 10 minutes more until the cannelloni is bubbling.

Linguine al Pomodoro

Pasta with homemade tomato sauce

Serves: 6
Cooking time: 10 minutes

Ingredients

1 packet of dried linguine pasta

12 fresh basil leaves

2 cups homemade sugo di pomodoro (tomato sauce)

300g fresh ricotta

freshly ground black pepper

extra virgin olive oil

Method

Fill a saucepan with water and bring to the boil. Add linguine and cook as per directions on the packet for serving size and cooking time. Cook until al dente. Drain. While pasta is cooking prepare sauce. Take a saucepan. Add basil leaves to the tomato pasta sauce and heat on low heat. Add half the ricotta cheese, pepper to taste and a drizzle of olive oil to the pan. Add sauce to cooked linguine. Add the rest of the ricotta in chunks and fresh basil leaves for garnish. Serve warm.

Pasta e Fagioli

In Italian this dish means 'pasta and beans'. A traditional Southern Italian dish which uses inexpensive ingredients.

Ingredients

1 small onion, chopped

6 cloves garlic, minced

2 sprigs fresh rosemary

1 tbsp tomato concentrate

1 stalk celery

1 cup chicken stock, no salt

1 can chopped Italian Roma tomatoes

500g dried cannellini or borlotti beans, soaked overnight, cooked 1 hour until tender then drained

1 tsp dried oregano

3 tbsp flat-leaf parsley

200g 'ditalini' or other small dried pasta tubes

3 tbsp olive oil

Method

Heat 2 tbsp olive oil in a heavy-based saucepan. Add onion and garlic. Cook until soft. Add celery and chicken stock. Stir well. Simmer covered for 5 minutes. Place 1/2 beans into a bowl. Mash with a fork. Then add to the saucepan.

Add tomatoes, remaining beans, pasta and oregano. Cover saucepan. Simmer on low heat for 10 - 15 minutes until pasta is cooked but still a little firm. Add parsley. Serve with warm crusty bread.

Potato Gnocchi with Sage Butter

Potato gnocchi is a favorite traditional dish in the North of Italy. Elsewhere in Italy, gnocchi is also made from pumpkin, semolina, polenta, spinach and ricotta.

Serves: 6
Cooking time: 45 minutes

Ingredients

1 kg starchy potatoes, peeled
2 large egg yolks
300g plain flour

Method

Cook potatoes in boiling water until tender, 20 minutes. Drain. Mash. Slowly stir in egg yolk and enough flour to make a soft dough.
Roll with your hands on a floured board and make a rope 1 cm in diameter. Cut off 2.5 cm pieces. Twist each one around the back of a fork to give

the gnocchi their grooves. Place the pieces on kitchen towels and set aside for 1 hour.

To cook gnocchi, bring water to a boil in a large saucepan. Place 20 - 24 gnocchi into the boiling water. Simmer for 2 minutes. Remove gently with a slotted spoon. Repeat until all gnocchi are cooked. Melt butter with sage leaves. Drizzle over the gnocchi. Add a grind of black pepper. Serve hot.

Pumpkin Gnocchi

Serves: 6 - 8
Cooking time: 30 minutes

Ingredients

1.5g pumpkin, peeled and chopped

450g plain flour

2 eggs, beaten

100g butter, melted

fresh basil leaves, torn, for garnish

black pepper, freshly ground

Method

Heat oven to 200 C. Place pumpkin on a greased baking tray. Bake until tender.

Place in a bowl and mash while still hot. Cool for 10 minutes. Add eggs, flour and mix until smooth and firm. Add more flour if needed.

Fill a large saucepan with water and bring to the boil. Shape dough into 2.5 cm balls. Drop them gently into water, a few at a time and cook for 2 - 3 minutes. Remove with slotted spoon and place in a serving bowl. When all gnocchi are cooked, drizzle with melted butter, add a grind of black pepper and basil leaves to garnish. Serve hot.

Gnocchi Ragu of Mushrooms

Serves: 4 - 6
Cooking time: 40 minutes

Ingredients

100g gnocchi

2 tbsp olive oil

2 medium onions, finely chopped

2 carrots, finely chopped

3 cloves garlic, crushed

1 400g can Italian tomatoes (no salt)

150 ml chicken stock (preferably homemade)

3 tbsp tomato paste (no salt added)

1 sprig fresh rosemary

500g brown mushrooms, cut in chunks.

Method

Bring water to boil and cook gnocchi 2 - 3 minutes. Drain. Heat oil in a pan. Add carrots, onions, garlic and cook until soft. Add tomatoes and simmer on low heat for 10 minutes. Add tomatoes, stock, tomato paste and rosemary. Simmer for 40 minutes.

Heat a frying pan with a little olive oil and 1 clove of crushed garlic. Add mushrooms. Cook until soft. To serve mix gnocchi together with sauce and place mushrooms on top. Serve warm.

Penne alla Arrabbiata

Tomatoes, chili and fresh basil go together to make a classic Italian dish.

Serves: 4 - 6
Cooking time: 20 minutes

Ingredients

2 whole cloves garlic, peeled

1 clove garlic, finely chopped

1 400g can Roma Italian tomatoes, no salt added

10 fresh basil leaves, stalks removed

1 dried red chili pepper

freshly ground black pepper

extra virgin olive oil

400g - 500g dried penne pasta

Method

Heat a frying pan with 3 tbsp olive oil. Add whole garlic and cook until the garlic turns golden brown. Remove garlic with slotted spoon and discard. Add chopped garlic and cook stirring for one minute taking care not to burn. Add tomatoes in their juice. Mash tomatoes with a wooden spoon. Cook on medium heat. Meanwhile wash basil and cut into thin strips. Take the red chili and cut in half. If you prefer a milder sauce, remove the seeds. Chop the chili. Add to pan with basil. Stir well. Add pepper to taste. Simmer on low heat while cooking the pasta. To cook pasta, fill a large saucepan with water and bring to a rolling boil. Add pasta. Cook until pasta is soft but still firm. Drain and place in a serving dish. Add the sauce and serve.

Spaghetti alla Aglio

This Roman garlic spaghetti recipe takes less than 20 minutes to prepare.

Serves: 4

Cooking time: 20 minutes

Ingredients

4 cloves garlic, finely chopped

200g - 300g finer Italian spaghetti (size 2 or 3)

1 tsp dried chili pepper flakes

4 tbsp flat-leaf parsley, roughly chopped

4 tbsp extra virgin olive oil

freshly ground black pepper

fresh basil leaves, shredded

Method

Cook spaghetti in boiling water until al dente. Drain in colander. Place olive oil in a frying pan with garlic and chili. Cook over low heat until the garlic is golden. Toss the pasta with warm garlic oil and parsley. Garnish with basil leaves and pepper.

Spaghetti alla Carbonara

This variation uses mushrooms instead of bacon.

Serves: 4
Cooking time: 15 minutes

Ingredients

4 eggs

1/4 cup cream

400g mushrooms, washed and sliced

freshly ground black pepper

2 tbsp flat-leaf parsley

300g dried spaghetti

extra virgin olive oil

Method

Fill a large saucepan with cold water and bring to
the boil. Meanwhile, heat oil in a frying pan. Add
mushrooms and cook slowly for 10 minutes until
soft. Remove mushrooms from pan. Set aside.
Drop spaghetti into boiling water. Cook following
instructions on the packet. Drain. Combine eggs

and cream. Place hot pasta in a bowl and add the egg and cream mixture. Toss together. Add mushrooms and parsley. Serve immediately.

S p a g h e t t i
w i t h   S q u i d

Serves: 4 - 6
Cooking time: 40 minutes

I n g r e d i e n t s

450g fresh squid, cleaned

400g dried spaghetti

1 small onion, minced

3 cloves garlic, finely chopped

1/3 cup dry white wine (optional)

1/4 cup olive oil

1 can diced Italian tomatoes, no salt

2 tsp tomato paste, no salt

1 bunch flat-leaf parsley, roughly chopped

red pepper flakes

1 lemon

1/4 cup fresh basil leaves, shredded

freshly ground black pepper

M e t h o d

Dice squid body and tentacles.

Heat oil in a pan. Add some red pepper flakes

(to taste), garlic and onion. Cook 2 minutes on medium heat until golden. Take care not to brown. Add squid and cook over a low heat stirring occasionally. Add tomato sauce, tomato paste, juice from 1/2 the lemon, a little grated zest of the lemon and wine to the pan. Add pepper. Simmer on low heat until the squid is tender, about 10 - 15 minutes, taking care not to overcook or squid will become rubbery. Cook spaghetti in boiling water until al dente. Drain. Place in a serving bowl and add squid sauce. Toss through parsley. Serve with lemon wedges.

Pasta al Pesto

A garlic and basil pasta from Liguria

Serves: 4
Cooking time: 30 minutes

Ingredients

1 large bunch of basil, about 45 leaves (no stalks)
2 cloves garlic
1/3 cup extra virgin olive oil
1/2 to 1 cup pine nuts
500g dried spaghetti
freshly ground black pepper

Method

Place garlic, pine nuts and basil leaves in a food processor. Process and add oil slowly in a steady stream. Take care not to over process. Add a little more oil if necessary to make a smooth, textured pesto. Next cook the pasta. Fill a saucepan with water and bring to the boil. Cook pasta according to instructions until al dente. Remove from heat. Drain. Place in serving bowls. Spoon pesto on top and toss through. Add ground pepper to taste.

FISH

Calamari Fritti

Serves: 4
Cooking time: 30 minutes

Ingredients

450g calamari, cleaned and cut into rings
2/3 cup plain flour
4 tbsp semolina
canola oil for frying
1 lemon, cut in wedges

Method

Wash calamari and dry on paper towels.
Heat oil in a fry pan. Beat eggs in one bowl. Place
flour in another bowl. Place semolina on a plate.
Dredge rings in flour. Dip floured calamari in egg
and then into the semolina. Fry in small batches
until golden. Drain on kitchen paper. Serve hot on
a plate with lemon wedges and a grind of black
pepper to taste.

Grilled Squid with Cannellini Beans

Serves: 4 - 6
Cooking time: 15 minutes

Ingredients:

1/2 cup olive oil

3 cloves garlic, finely chopped

2 tbsp flat leaf parsley, chopped

1 tsp fresh marjoram, chopped

1 tsp fresh thyme

juice of 1 lemon or lime

freshly ground black pepper

500 - 750g cleaned calamari (squid) bodies, dried on kitchen paper

1 cup of cooked cannellini beans (or can no-added salt beans, drained and rinsed)

5 cups of rocket leaves, or assorted salad greens

2 medium carrots, peeled and cut in thin strips

1 yellow capsicum (yellow bell pepper) in thin strips

Method

Heat olive oil in a frying pan. Add garlic and cook for 30 seconds taking care not to burn. Add lemon juice and pepper. Set dressing aside.

Heat grill to hot or prepare barbeque. Take 2 tbsp. of the lemon dressing and brush over the squid before cooking. Bring black pepper over the squid. Cook squid 2 minutes each side taking care not to overcook or the squid will turn rubbery. Cool. Cut across each tube to make 1 cm wide rings. Set aside. Place beans, carrots, rocket and yellow pepper into a bowl. Toss well with the rest of the lemon dressing. Spoon onto a serving plate and add the cooked squid. Serve at room temperature with crusty bread.

Salmon and Orange Salad

Serves: 6
Cooking time: 30 minutes

Ingredients

500g boneless salmon fillets

black pepper, freshly ground

1 large orange

1 avocado

1 tbsp orange zest

6 tbsp orange juice

3 tbsp extra virgin olive oil

2 tbsp mint leaves

mixed baby salad leaves

Method

Heat oven to 200 C. Place salmon on a lightly oiled baking try. Bake for 10 minutes. Set aside. Make the salad. Cut peel off orange and cut into segments. Place orange zest, juice, olive oil and pepper in a bowl and whisk together.

Break salmon into chunks and add to the dressing.

Toss gently. Add orange segments and mint to the bowl. Toss lightly. Place on top of washed salad leaves. Add slices of avocado and serve.

Tonno alla Palermitana

Grilled tuna in rosemary and garlic is a Palermo style of cooking fish. You can use any white fish instead of tuna.

Serves: 4 - 6
Cooking time: 1 hour

Ingredients

6 fresh tuna steaks or 750g to 1kg firm white fish

1 cup dry white wine

4 fresh sage leaves, finely chopped

1 sprig fresh rosemary, finely chopped

2 cloves garlic, finely chopped

juice of 2 lemons or 1 lime

1/4 cup flat-leaf parsley, finely chopped

1/2 cup extra virgin olive oil

freshly ground black pepper

Method

Mix wine, sage, rosemary and garlic together.
Place fish in a flat (non metal) dish. Pour marinade

over fish. Cover and refrigerate for 1 hour, turning often. Mix lemon juice and parsley together and set aside. Heat barbeque or oven grill on high. Drain fish. Save marinade from the fish. Dry tuna on kitchen paper. Dip into olive oil and pepper. Place fish on barbeque or under the oven grill. Cook, basting with the wine marinade and parsley and lemon mixture, until the fish starts to look blackened and cooked. About 3 minutes each side. Serve hot.

Breaded Ocean Fish

Serves: 4

Ingredients

200g plain white flour

3 eggs

black pepper, freshly ground

400g breadcrumbs, or polenta

1/2 bunch, flat-leaf parsley, chopped finely

1/2 bunch mint, stalks removed, chopped finely

finely grated zest of one lemon

4 x 200g fish pieces

1 bunch rocket

fresh basil leaves

4 ripe tomatoes, roughly chopped

6 tbsp extra virgin olive oil

3 tbsp lemon juice

olive oil for frying

1 lemon, cut into wedges for garnish

Method

Place flour on a plate. Place eggs in a bowl and whisk well. Place breadcrumbs on a plate and season with pepper, mint, lemon zest and parsley. Make a dressing in a screw top jar by combining lemon juice, olive oil and pepper. Shake. Place rocket and tomatoes on a plate. Pour dressing over. Set aside. Prepare fish. Dip each fillet into flour, then egg and then breadcrumbs.

Heat some oil in a frying pan and cook fish over medium heat. Turn over and cook until each side is golden brown and the fish is cooked. Drain on kitchen towels. Place on top of the salad and garnish with lemon wedges.

Insalata Fruitta di Mare

Seafood salad from the Amalfi coast.

Serves: 6 - 8
Cooking time: 30 minutes

Ingredients

4 tbsp olive oil

4 cloves garlic, chopped

8 scallops,

500g squid rings and tentacles, cleaned

1/2 tsp freshly ground black pepper

25 raw shrimp, peeled and deveined

1 red capsicum, deseeded, sliced thinly

1 yellow capsicum deseeded, sliced thinly

1 red onion, sliced thinly

1 small fennel (white part only)

zest of one lemon

1 lemon, juiced

1/2 cup flat-leaf parsley, roughly chopped

Method

Place 2 tbsp olive oil in a frying pan. Add garlic
and cook on medium flame until garlic turns
golden. Take care not to brown the garlic.
Turn heat to high. Add scallops. Sauté 2 minutes.
Remove scallops and set aside. Add shrimps. Sauté
until they turn pink taking care not to overcook.
Add shrimps to the bowl of scallops. Add calamari
rings and tentacles to the pan and cook until
tender (about 3 to 5 minutes). Add to the scallops
and shrimp. Add a grinding of pepper to the
seafood. Mix through. Add olive oil, pepper, onions,
fennel, lemon juice, lemon zest and parsley to the
seafood. Toss well and place on a serving platter.
Serve warm or place in fridge and let flavors
develop overnight before serving.

Scabeggio

Fish marinated in wine, lemon and sage. Keeps a week in the fridge for quick meals.

Serves: 4
Cooking time: 15 minutes

Ingredients

500g fresh white fish

100g white flour

2 cloves garlic, finely chopped

sprig of fresh sage

1/2 cup olive oil

1/2 cup white wine

1 red onion, sliced into rings

2 tbsp Italian parsley, finely chopped

1 tbsp lemon juice

1/4 tsp black pepper

Method

Flour fish fillets. Heat oil in a pan and fry fish in a little oil until golden and cooked. Remove from heat and drain on kitchen paper.

Place fish in a shallow serving dish. Add garlic,

onion rings and sage on top of the fish. Place oil
and white wine in a bowl and whisk. Add lemon
juice and black pepper. Pour marinade over fish.
Cover and leave to marinate for 1 hour minimum.
Serve as an appetizer with crusty bread. Bring to
room temperature before serving.

Salmon Fettuccine

Serves: 4 - 6
Cooking time: 15 minutes

Ingredients

500g fresh salmon, skinned and boned
5 ripe tomatoes
400g dried fettuccine pasta
freshly ground pepper
1 lemon
1 tsp grated lemon zest
rocket salad leaves

Method

Cook the pasta in boiling water according to directions on the packet. While pasta is cooking , cut salmon into 2cm cubes. Place olive oil, salmon, lemon zest and pepper in a frying pan. Cook gently until the salmon turns pink. Add lemon juice and rocket leaves. Toss. When the pasta is cooked, drain and add to the salmon. Toss and serve.

MEAT

Osso Buco

A Milanese version of veal shanks braised in vegetables and wine gravy.

Serves: 6 - 8
Cooking time: 90 minutes

Ingredients

6 pieces of osso buco (veal shanks)

1 large brown onion, chopped finely

2 medium sized carrots, peeled, chopped

3 cloves of garlic, peeled and crushed

1 bay leaf

1 pinch saffron

1 bulb fennel, white part only, sliced

1 sprig fresh rosemary

1/4 tsp dried juniper berries

plain flour

1 can crushed Italian tomatoes (no salt)

olive oil

freshly ground black pepper, unsalted butter

1/4 cup red wine

1/2 cup water

Method

Place flour on a plate. Season with freshly ground black pepper. Dredge the meat in the flour. Place an ovenproof casserole dish on low heat. Add 2 tbsp olive oil and 1 tbsp unsalted butter. When the butter is melted turn the heat to medium high. Add meat. Brown well. Add onions, garlic and carrots. Cook until the vegetables are starting to brown. Add wine, tomatoes, saffron, bay leaf, juniper berries, fennel and water. When simmering remove the casserole from the cooktop and cover. Cook in a 180 degree C oven for 1 1/2 hours or until the meat is tender and falling away from the bone. Add more water if the gravy appears too dry. Serve hot with mashed potatoes.

Agnello alla Griglia

Grilled lamb with rosemary and lemon

Serves: 4
Cooking time: 10 minutes

Ingredients

4 x 200g lamb chops or cutlets

100ml olive oil

4 cloves garlic, minced

4 sprigs fresh rosemary

black pepper, freshly ground

2 lemons, cut in half, rocket leaves

Method

Cut fat off lamb. Place in a flat dish. Tear rosemary leaves off the stalk. Mix with garlic, pepper and olive oil. Pour over the meat. Marinade for 2 hours in the fridge. Heat barbeque to high. Place lamb on the grill. Cook 5 minutes each side or until meat is cooked. Place on a bed of rocket and squeeze lemon over before serving.

Medaglioni di Maiale

Pork and basil tenderloin

Serves: 4 - 8
Cooking time: 30 minutes

Ingredients

1 small pork tenderloin

4 tbsp olive oil

2 cloves garlic, crushed

4 tbsp flour for coating

white pepper, ground

1 cup homemade dried breadcrumbs

1 egg

8 fresh basil leaves

homemade mozzarella, cut in 8 thin slices

freshly ground black pepper

Method

Cut pork into 1 1/2 cm slices. Place flour on a plate. Season with white pepper. Beat egg in a small bowl. Place breadcrumbs on a plate. Lightly dip pork into flour, then egg, then breadcrumbs. When all pork pieces are prepared, heat oil in a frying pan. Sauté garlic until golden. Remove garlic from pan and discard. Brown pork for 3 minutes on each side in the garlic oil. Place on a baking sheet. Top with basil and a slice of mozzarella. Grill until cheese melts, about two minutes. Serve warm.

Roast Pork with Fig Sauce

Serves: 6 - 8
Cooking time: 50 minutes

Roast Pork

Ingredients

2 tbsp olive oil

2 tbsp chopped fresh rosemary

black pepper, freshly ground to taste

1.7 - 2 kg boneless pork loin or leg

1 cup home made chicken stock

Method

Heat oven to 200 C. Mix oil, rosemary and pepper together in a bowl. Place pork in a baking pan. Cover the pork with the oil and rosemary mixture. Roast for 45 minutes or until cooked, turning the pork every 15 minutes until all the sides are brown. Remove from oven. Cover with foil and let rest for 10 minutes. While the roast is sitting, place the baking tray on a medium heat. Add chicken stock, scrape the pan and stir well. Bring the gravy to a simmer. Carve the meat into 1cm slices. Arrange on a large serving plate and spoon the warmed fig sauce over the meat. Serve.

Fig Sauce

Ingredients

2 cups no salt chicken stock

10 dried figs

2 sprigs of rosemary

2 cinnamon sticks

2 tbsp unsalted butter

1 tbsp liquid honey

freshly ground black pepper

Method

Heat chicken broth, figs, cinnamon, rosemary and honey in a large saucepan. Boil on medium heat for 20 minutes or until the liquid reduces by half. Strain and discard the rosemary and cinnamon. Cool. Blend with butter and pepper to a puree. Cover and set aside. You can make this sauce a day ahead and reheat on low heat.

No Salt Pork and Beef Sausages

Made without eggs, flour, bread, additives, preservatives, salt or skins.

Makes: 16 sausages
Cooking time: 10 minutes

Ingredients

500g minced lean beef or veal

250g minced pork

2 cloves garlic, minced

1/4 tsp nutmeg

1/4 tsp allspice

pinch of cloves

1 tsp paprika

pinch of cayenne pepper

1/4 tsp ground white or black pepper

1 tbsp olive oil

Method

Place meat in a bowl with spices, and garlic. Mix together well. Wet hands and shape into sausage shapes. Heat barbeque or oven grill. Brush sausages with oil. Grill, turning to brown all sides.

No Salt Classic Italian Sausages

Makes: 16 sausages
Cooking time: 45 minutes

Ingredients

1.3 kg pork shoulder or rump cut into 2 inch pieces

2 tbsp garlic, minced

1 1/2 tsp fennel seeds, toasted

1 tbsp. freshly ground black pepper

1/2 tsp anise seeds, ground

3 tbsp paprika, optional

2 tbsp flat-leaf parsley leaves, chopped

3 tbsp red wine, or meat stock

pinch of cayenne pepper

Method

Place meats in a bowl with spices, and garlic. Mix together well. Refrigerate overnight in a covered bowl. Pass meat mixture through a meat grinder or use a food processor and process until the mixture is finely ground. Test to adjust season by frying a tsp.

in a little olive oil. Adjust seasoning if needed. Wet hands and shape into sausage shapes. Heat barbeque or oven grill. Brush sausages with oil. Grill turning to brown all sides. Uncooked mixture will keep up to 3 days in the fridge or store in the freezer for up to 3 months.

Arrosto di Maiale al Limone

Lemon sage pork chops

Serves: 4
Cooking time: 40 minutes

Ingredients

4 pork chops, trimmed of fat

1 lemon, juiced and zested

3 cloves garlic, crushed

1 sprig sage

1 bay leaf

freshly ground white pepper

1/2 cup vegetable stock (see recipe for stock)

Method

Place flour on a plate. Dip pork chops into flour. Heat olive oil in a large casserole. Add garlic, bay leaf, lemon zest and juice, sage, garlic, pepper and stock. Cover with lid and bake in a 180 degree C oven for 30 minutes. Serve with warm polenta.

Pork
with Prunes

A rustic dish of pork, prunes and grain mustard.

Serves: 4
Cooking time: 10 minutes

Ingredients

8 prunes, soaked in water

2 tbsp olive oil

2 tbsp unsalted butter

4 x 240g pork chops, or pork tenderloin steaks

175 ml dry white wine

175 ml water or homemade stock

2 tsp grain mustard

freshly ground black pepper

Method

Heat oil and butter in frying pan over high heat.
Place pork chops into the pan and cook both
sides. Remove from heat, cover with foil. Place in a
warm oven. Add wine and mustard to the juices in
pan. Add drained prunes. Stir to combine with the

pan juices. Season with pepper. Remove pork from oven and pour the sauce over. Serve with polenta or mashed potatoes.

De Sarno's Lasagna

Perfect for a big family get together.

Serves: 12 - 18
Cooking time: 50 minutes

Ingredients

500g lasagna noodles

500g ground beef

500g minced pork

1 large onion, chopped, 4 cloves garlic

2 tsp sugar

1 1/2 tsp dried basil

1/2 tsp fennel seeds

1/4 tsp black pepper

200g mushrooms, sliced

400g can Italian tomatoes, chopped

2 (170g) cans tomato paste

850g homemade ricotta cheese

1 tbsp fresh parley, chopped

900g homemade mozzarella cheese, shredded

2 eggs, beaten

Method

Prepare lasagna according to packet directions. Drain and set aside. Cook beef and pork. Drain off fat. Add onion, garlic and mushrooms to meat mixture. Cook until onion is soft. Add sugar, basil, fennel, pepper, tomatoes and tomato paste. Mix well. Simmer 1 hour. Combine eggs, ricotta, parsley in a bowl. Mix well. Grease the bottom of a large rectangular baking dish, spread enough meat to cover. Layer lasagna noodles, then meat sauce, ricotta mixture and mozzarella cheese. Repeat layering making sure to end up with a lasagna noodle layer. Sprinkle with mozzarella.

Cover dish with foil. Bake at 190 degrees C for 25 minutes. Remove foil and bake for a further 25 minutes until golden and cooked. Cut into squares.

Classic Italian Lasagna

Serves: 6 - 8
Cooking time: 30 minutes

Red Sauce

Ingredients

2 tbsp olive oil

1 tbsp unsalted butter

4 cloves garlic, finely chopped

1 medium onion, chopped

225g mushrooms, chopped

200g can tomato puree

2 tbsp tomato paste

2 400g cans diced tomatoes

2 tsp Italian herbs or mix dried oregano and basil

1/2 tsp black pepper, ground

White sauce

Ingredients

3 cups milk

5 tbsp flour

4 tbsp unsalted butter

1/2 tsp white pepper

Lasagna

Ingredients

12 no-cook lasagna sheets (I use Barilla brand)

450g minced beef

450g mozzarella cheese

Method

Heat oven to 180 degrees C.

Grease a large baking dish with olive oil.

In a large frying pan brown minced beef over medium heat. Drain fat and set aside. In a medium saucepan, over medium heat, add 2 tbsp olive oil and 1 tbsp unsalted butter. Add garlic and cook for 2 minutes. Add onion and mushrooms. Cook until soft. Add tomatoes and tomato paste, Italian herbs and pepper. Stir to combine. Cover and simmer over low heat for 30 minutes. Add cooked beef and simmer. While sauce is simmering prepare the white sauce. Melt 4 tbsp butter and add flour while stirring for 2 minutes. Slowly add milk using a whisk to ensure the sauce is smooth. Cook while whisking for 5 minutes making sure sauce does not stick to the pan bottom. Once sauce thickens remove from heat. Assemble lasagna as follows. You will have three layers of noodles as well as sauces and cheese, so keep in mind to split the sauces, noodles and cheeses into three so you don't run out during assembly of the lasagna.

Place four lasagna sheets on the bottom of the pan. Layer the red sauce, white sauce and mozzarella spreading all to the edges. Add another layer of lasagna sheets, red sauce, white sauce and mozzarella and top with a final sheet of lasagna noodles. Layer the red sauce, white sauce and cheese again. Cover lasagna with tin foil and bake for 30 minutes. Remove foil and let lasagna sit for 15 minutes before cutting and serving.

Ragu Napolentano

A traditional Southern Italian family lunch.

Serves: 8 - 10
Cooking time: 2 hours

Ingredients

500g pork ribs

250g veal, cut in chunks

500g beef topside, cut in cubes

1 small onion, finely chopped

4 tbsp extra virgin olive oil

2 tbsp tomato paste diluted in 100ml red wine

3 x 400g cans chopped Italian tomatoes, no salt

pinch hot chili flakes

handful fresh basil leaves, stalks removed

freshly ground black pepper

Method

Heat oil in a casserole on the cooktop. Add onion, beef, pork, veal and cook on high heat until the meat is seared. About 10 minutes.

Add wine and tomato paste. Stir for 5 minutes until wine evaporates and meat turns brown. Add tomatoes and chili flakes. Reduce heat, cover and simmer for 2 hours, stirring from time to time. Check that there is enough liquid. Add a little more wine or water it necessary. Sauce will be thick and aromatic. Skim fat before serving. Add freshly ground black pepper.

Bistecca Fiorentina

Serves: 4
Cooking time: 10 minutes

Ingredients

500g - 1kg porterhouse cut 5cm thick

black pepper

1 sprig fresh thyme

2 cups rocket salad leaves

2 cloves garlic, minced

2 tbsp olive oil

juice 1 lemon

Method

Prepare hot grill. Place steak directly on fire. Turn. Brush with rosemary. When cooked, remove from heat. Toss rocket with garlic, lemon juice, a dash of olive oil and pepper to taste. Carve steak into diagonal slices. Place meat on salad. Serve.

Chicken with Herb Sauce

Chicken served with Italy's famous green sauce.

Serves: 6
Cooking time: 20 minutes

Ingredients:

6 chicken breasts, skin on

2 tbsp olive oil

black pepper, freshly ground

Salsa verde

1 cup flat-leaf parsley

1 cup fresh basil leaves, no stalks

2 cloves garlic, finely chopped

1 tbsp. red wine vinegar

5 tbsp. extra virgin olive oil

Method

Place the basil and garlic in a food processor.
Blend. Add the garlic, vinegar and pepper. Blend.
Slowly add a stream of olive oil while the motor is

running. Add a little water if needed to make a pouring sauce. Prepare chicken by rubbing the pieces with olive oil. Place on a barbeque or under a grill. Cook slowly until cooked. About 15 - 20 minutes, turning to brown both sides. Slice chicken and place on serving plates. Spoon salsa verde over the top. Serve with crispy roasted potatoes (with rosemary or roasted garlic).

Fettuccine
with Chicken

Serves: 6 - 8
Cooing time: 10 minutes

Ingredients

2 tbsp olive oil

2 cloves garlic, crushed

1 small brown onion, finely chopped

250g brown or button mushrooms, thinly sliced

1 cup cream

50g butter

500g dried fettuccine pasta

300g cooked chicken, shredded

1/2 cup walnuts, roasted and chopped roughly

1/2 cup flat-leaf parsley, roughly chopped

1/4 cup fresh basil, shredded

black pepper, freshly ground

30g homemade mozzarella

Method

Cook pasta in a large saucepan according to directions on the packet. Meanwhile, heat oil in a large frying pan. Add onions and garlic. Cook for 3 minutes until transparent, taking care not to brown. Add mushrooms and cook, stirring the pan, until tender. Add cream and black pepper. Bring to boil. Turn heat to low and simmer for 3 minutes then add butter. When pasta is al dente (firm but tender) drain and return to the saucepan. Add hot cream sauce with chicken, walnuts and parsley. Toss gently. Serve with shredded basil leaves, pepper to taste and grated mozzarella.

Pollo alla Cacciatora

Braised 'hunters chicken'

Serves: 6 - 8
Cooking time: 1hour 10minutes

Ingredients

1 tbsp extra virgin olive oil

1 fresh chicken, cut into 8 pieces

2 cloves garlic, crushed

450g fresh brown, mushrooms cut in cubes

1 medium onion, finely sliced

1 tsp fresh rosemary leaves

2 stalks celery, finely chopped

2 medium carrots, chopped

1/2 cup white wine

1 cup homemade chicken stock

1 can Italian tomatoes, no salt

2 bay leaves

1/2 tsp sugar

Fresh flat-leaf parley for garnish

Method

Heat oil in a large saucepan. Add garlic, onions, celery and carrots.

Cook for 5 - 10 minutes, stirring occasionally to prevent burning. Add chicken and cook on medium heat, to brown the chicken.

Add wine, chicken stock, tomatoes, bay leaves and sugar. Place lid on pan and simmer on low heat for 20 minutes covered, then 15 - 20 minutes uncovered until the chicken is tender. Remove from heat. Add freshly ground pepper, chopped flat leaf parsley and garlic. Serve with potatoes roasted with fresh rosemary.

Pollo
alla Bruno

This is a simple, delicious way to roast chicken.

Serves: 6 - 8
Cooking time: 1 hour

Ingredients

2 kg whole chicken

100g fresh rosemary, chopped roughly

3 fresh bay leaves or 5 dried

1 large brown onion, chopped

2 lemons, sliced, skin on

4 large potatoes, or sweet potatoes, sliced

juice of 2 lemons

100ml balsamic vinegar

freshly ground white or black pepper

Method

Heat oven to 220 C.

Place rosemary, onion, bay leaves, lemon juice,
lemon slices, pepper and balsamic vinegar into a
large roasting pan or ovenproof dish. Sprinkle with

1/4 cup of water. Place chicken on top. Drizzle with olive oil. Sprinkle with freshly ground pepper. Place chicken in a hot oven and bake for 30 - 45 minutes or until cooked. In the last 10 minutes of cooking, add a lid of kitchen foil if the chicken appears too brown. Remove from oven when cooked and test by pushing a skewer into the base of a leg to check if chicken cooked. If the juices run clear the chicken is cooked. If not return to the oven and cook a further 10 minutes and test again.

Remove chicken from the oven. Cut into serving pieces. Place on a serving plate with potatoes and onions. Drain fat from baking tray. Place on low heat. Add juice of lemon and ¼ cup of water. Stir while scraping the tray. Pour the lemon gravy over the chicken and serve.

Barbequed Chicken Legs

Prepare the marinade the day before so the flavor comes through.

Serves: 4

Ingredient

chicken legs

4 cloves of garlic, crushed

150ml balsamic vinegar

150 ml olive oil

1/2 bunch fresh marjoram, chopped

black pepper, freshly ground

1 lemon, cut in wedges

Method

Place garlic, oil, balsamic vinegar, herbs and pepper in a bowl. Whisk together. Pour over chicken legs and leave covered overnight in fridge. Turn occasionally. Heat barbeque, grill chicken. Remove from heat and serve warm with lemon wedges and grilled mushrooms and corn.

Italian Lemon Herb Chicken

Serves: 6 - 8
Cooking time: 30 minutes

Ingredients

8 chicken pieces

1/4 cup lemon juice

3 cloves garlic, crushed

1 tsp fresh rosemary leaves, chopped

2 tbsp fresh oregano leaves, chopped

2 tbsp fresh flat-leaf parsley

2 tbsp thinly sliced fresh basil leaves

2 shallots, finely chopped

black pepper

Method

Place chicken pieces in a flat dish. Mix all ingredients together and pour over the chicken. Marinade overnight in the fridge. Barbeque chicken, bake at 180 degrees C,or grill.

VEGETABLES

Fennel and Orange Salad

A crunchy fresh citrus salad.

Serves: 4
Cooking time: 10 minutes

Ingredients

2 oranges, peeled, sliced into rounds
1 medium fennel, washed, white part only
2 brown shallots, peeled, finely sliced
ground white pepper
2 tsp extra virgin olive oil

Method

Using a sharp knife, slice the fennel thinly.
Place in bowl. Add shallots. Add olive oil and
pepper. Mix well. Place in a serving bowl and leave
to sit for 30 minutes. Drizzle with olive oil. Serve.

Insalata Caprese

A simple salad made with freshly sliced tomatoes, mozzarella and fresh basil.

Serves: 6
Cooking time: 10 minutes

Ingredients

2 balls of low salt mozzarella, sliced 1 cm thick

5 ripe Roma tomatoes, sliced 1 cm thick

12 fresh basil leaves

extra virgin olive oil

black pepper, freshly ground

Method

Arrange tomatoes and mozzarella on a plate by alternating slices. Place a fresh basil leaf between each slice. Drizzle with olive oil. Grind black pepper over the salad and serve.

Condigiun

Salad made with tomatoes, peppers, cucumber, basil, boiled egg, garlic and tuna.

Serves: 4 - 6
Cooking time: 10 minutes

Ingredients

I can tuna in oil, no salt added, drained

4 ripe acid-free tomatoes, chopped

freshly ground black pepper

1/2 red onion, chopped

1 cucumber, peeled and chopped

10 fresh basil leaves, whole

2 hard-boiled eggs cut in quarters

1 red capsicum (sweet bell pepper) cut in chunks

Method

Toss all ingredients (except egg and basil) together with balsamic dressing. Place in a serving bowl. Garnish with egg slices and fresh basil leaves.

For the dressing

Ingredients

6 tbsp extra virgin oil

3 tbsp balsamic vinegar

1 pinch sugar

freshly ground black pepper

1 clove garlic, crushed

Method

Place ingredients in a small screw-top container.
Shake together before serving over salad.

Peperonata

A stew of onions, sweet peppers and tomatoes.

Serves: 4
Cooking time: 30 minutes

Ingredients

2 medium sweet red peppers, cut into strips

1 large sweet yellow pepper, cut into strips

1 large brown onion, thinly sliced

8 ripe Italian plum tomatoes, chopped

1 pinch of sugar

freshly ground black pepper

1 bunch fresh basil

40 ml olive oil

Method

Place oil in a pan and add onions. Cook over medium heat until soft. Add red and yellow peppers. Add tomatoes. Cook for 30 minutes over low heat, stirring occasionally. Season with sugar, pepper and add basil leaves. Serve hot with crusty bread or as a pasta sauce topping. Delicious cold in sandwiches. Keeps for two days in the fridge.

Caponata

A Sicilian dish of aubergines and celery in a tasty sweet and sour sauce.

Serves: 6 - 8
Cooking time: 30 minutes

Ingredients

4 medium eggplants, cut into 2cm cubes

1 medium Spanish red onion, chopped

6 Italian plum tomatoes, finely chopped

1 tbsp tomato paste

2 cloves garlic, finely chopped

1 celery stalk, finely chopped

1/2 cup extra virgin olive oil

1/4 cup pine nuts, toasted

3 tbsp dried currants

1 tsp dried red pepper flakes

2 tbsp sugar

1 tsp cinnamon

2 tsp fresh thyme leaves

6 sprigs mint, stalks removed, leaves chopped

1/4 cup balsamic vinegar

1 tsp unsweetened coca powder
freshly ground black pepper

Method

Heat 2 tbsp of oil in a large frying pan. Add onion, garlic and celery. Cook over medium heat stirring constantly until soft, about 5 minutes. Remove from pan and set aside.

Clean the pan and add 2 tbsp olive oil. Heat on high. Add eggplant and cook for 2 minutes. Turn eggplant over. Cook for 2 minutes. Keep turning the eggplant over, stirring all the time for 5 minutes. Then add onion mixture, tomatoes, tomato paste, cocoa powder, sugar, mint leaves, pine nuts and red pepper flakes. Cook until eggplant is soft, about 8 minutes. Remove from heat.

Place in a serving bowl. Season with pepper. Serve at room temperature with toasted bread or as a warm vegetable side dish to accompany chicken and beef. Can be stored in the fridge, covered, up to 5 days.

Ricotta Spinach Lasagna

Serves: 6
Cooking time: 1 hour

Ingredients

1 kg spinach leaves, washed and trimmed

3 eggs, lightly beaten

2 cups ricotta cheese

1 brown onion, finely chopped

1 1/2 cups Italian tomato sauce

8 fresh basil leaves, shredded

12 sheets lasagna

1 cup sliced mozzarella cheese

Method

Heat oven to 180 C. Grease a large shallow ovenproof dish. Place spinach leaves in boiling water, turn down heat to medium and cook until leaves are just wilted, taking care not to overcook. Remove from heat. Drain in a colander. When cool, squeeze liquid from the spinach using your hands. Add basil leaves. Chop roughly. Combine spinach and basil with egg and onion in a large bowl. Add freshly ground black pepper to season. Spread half the tomato sauce in the bottom of the baking dish. Cover with 3 sheets of lasagna. Top with 1/3 spinach mixture. Cover with 3 lasagna sheets; repeat layers finishing with remaining sauce and sprinkle with mozzarella. Cover with foil. Bake 30 minutes. Remove foil and bake for 10 minutes or until golden brown.

Sautéed Spinach

Serves: 4 - 6

Ingredients

2 kg baby spinach
100ml olive oil
4 cloves garlic, crushed
black pepper freshly ground
1 lemon

Method

Place spinach in a saucepan of boiling water and simmer for 4 minutes, until the spinach is tender. Take care not to overcook. Drain in a colander and squeeze out the excess water. Heat a frying pan. Add oil and garlic. Cook over low heat until garlic softens taking care not to brown or the garlic will taste bitter. Add spinach and cook for 4 minutes. Place in a serving dish and season with pepper. Squeeze juice of a lemon over spinach and serve.

Melanzane a Scapece

A marinated eggplant dish that is best made the day ahead.

Serves: 6 - 8
Cooking time: 30 minutes

Ingredients

4 small eggplants (aubergine)

1/4 cup extra virgin olive oil

3 cloves garlic, finely chopped

2 tsp fresh oregano

1 tsp dried red chili flakes

1 tbsp white wine vinegar

freshly ground black pepper

Method

Peel eggplants and cut in half. Place in salted boiling water for 10 minutes.

Remove and drain. Press with kitchen towels to remove excess moisture. Cut eggplant into slices and place in a serving bowl. Combine remaining ingredients and mix together into a dressing. Pour over the eggplant. Cover and place in the fridge. Leave 24 hours before serving as a relish.

Insalata di Broccolini

Serves: 4
Cooking time: 10 minutes

Ingredients

3 ripe tomatoes, chopped

black pepper, freshly ground

1 lemon, juiced

8 leaves of fresh oregano, finely chopped

6 tbsp. extra virgin olive oil

1 bunch broccolini

3 tbsp red wine vinegar

1/2 bunch flat-leaf parsley

8 fresh basil leaves

Method

Place tomatoes in a bowl. Add pepper, lemon juice, oil, and oregano. Mix together. Set aside. Cook broccolini in boiling water until firm and tender, 4 minutes. Take care not to overcook. Drain and place in a serving dish. Add tomato mixture. Add wine vinegar, parsley and basil.

Frittata

Serve this egg and vegetable dish at room temperature with a tossed green salad.

Serves: 6 - 8
Cooking time: 10 minutes

Ingredients

75ml olive oil

1 large red onion, finely chopped

2 garlic cloves, smashed

freshly ground black pepper

1 ripe tomato, chopped finely

3 zucchini, grated finely

6 - 8 fresh basil leaves, finely shredded

1 small bunch flat-leaf parsley, chopped roughly

Method

Heat oil in a heavy frying pan. Add onions and garlic and cook until transparent, taking care not to brown. Remove from heat.

Break eggs into a bowl and whisk seasoning with freshly ground black pepper. Add tomatoes, basil, zucchini and parsley. Add onions and mix together.

Wipe out frying pan and heat 1tbsp olive oil on medium heat. Add egg mixture to the pan. Cook gently checking to see if the underneath is starting to brown. Remove from cooktop and place pan under a low grill. Cool. When at room temperature, release the sides of the frittata using a spatula around the edge. Place a plate on top of the frittata and flip it over. Cut in wedges to serve.

Tiella
di Verdure

Sliced potatoes and egg plant

Serves: 4
Cooking time: 40 minutes

Ingredients

2 large courgettes (zucchini) cut into 5mm slices

4 medium Italian Roma (acid-free) tomatoes

6 large potatoes, peeled and cut into 3mm slices

1 large aubergine, cut into 3mm slices

1 large onion, thinly sliced

14 tbsp olive oil

3 tbsp fresh Italian parsley chopped

3 tbsp fresh basil, chopped

1/2 cup mozzarella cheese, grated

1 tbsp balsamic vinegar

Method

Heat grill. Brush aubergine and courgette with 2
tbsp olive oil and grill for 4 - 5 minutes until lightly
browned. Parboil potatoes for 5 minutes. Drain and

set aside. Heat 1 tbsp olive oil in a frying pan. Add onion and cook until soft. Remove from pan and set aside. Mix 8 tbsp olive oil with parsley, basil and season with freshly ground black pepper. Set aside. To assemble, place overlapping potato slices on the bottom of a large baking dish. Brush potatoes with herb oil. Add a layer of aubergine. Brush with herb oil. Add a layer of courgette. Brush with herb oil. Add a layer of tomato. Brush with herb oil. Add a layer of onion. Brush with herb oil. Repeat the process until all the vegetables are layered finishing with a top layer of potato. Mix 60g breadcrumbs with 1/2 cup mozzarella cheese and sprinkle over the top. Bake in the oven for 20 - 30 minutes until the vegetables are cooked and the top is golden.

Melanzane alla Menta

Eggplant, mint and garlic, create a delicious piquant taste.

Serves: 4 - 6
Cooking time: 10 minutes

Ingredients

2 eggplants cut into bite-sized chunks

1 onion, chopped

2 cloves garlic, finely chopped

1 small bunch fresh mint, finely chopped

1 small bunch flat-leaf parsley, finely chopped

squeeze of lemon, to taste

pinch or two of powdered cinnamon

freshly ground black pepper, olive oil for frying

Method

Heat oil in a frying pan. Add eggplant and ground pepper. Cook quickly. Then add onion and garlic together with mint and parsley. Add a squeeze of lemon and a couple of pinches of cinnamon.

Roasted Vegetable Lasagna

Serves: 6 - 8
Cooking time: 30 - 45 minutes

Ingredients

1 yellow sweet pepper (capsicum)

2 red sweet peppers (capsicum)

2 large aubergines (eggplants)

2 medium courgettes (zucchini) cut into chunks

1 small onion, peeled and cut into quarters

2 cloves garlic

1 cup pumpkin, cut into small chunks

8 tbsp olive oil

300g lasagna sheets

125g homemade mozzarella

3 Roma ripe acid free tomatoes, sliced

1 tsp oregano

1 tbsp fresh basil, chopped, ground black pepper

1 quantity homemade tomato sauce

1 quantity white sauce

White sauce

Ingredients

80g unsalted butter

80g plain white flour

750ml milk

Method

Melt butter in a saucepan. Stir in flour. Cook for 2 minutes. Slowly whisk in milk stirring constantly to prevent lumps. Bring to boil then turn heat down. Cook until sauce thickens and coats the back of a wooden stirring spoon. Remove from heat. Cool.

For the tomato sauce

Ingredients

1 onion, chopped

1 tbsp olive oil

1 stalk celery, finely chopped

2 cloves garlic, finely chopped

400g can chopped no salt tomatoes

1 tsp sugar

Method

Heat oil in a pan and add onion and garlic. Cook for 5 minutes until soft. Add celery and cook for 1 minute. Add tomatoes and sugar. Reduce heat and simmer uncovered for 30 minutes, stirring occasionally, until sauce thickens. Season with black pepper. Set aside

For the lasagna

Method

Heat oven to 200 degrees C.

Wash peppers, cut in half. Deseed. Then cut into large chunks. Cut ends off aubergines. Cut into 1/2cm slices. Grease a large baking tray with olive oil. Place pepper, aubergines, zucchini, onion and pumpkin on the tray. Toss with olive oil. Season with pepper. Roast in the oven for 20 minutes or until vegetables are lightly browned. Remove from oven. Set aside. Reduce oven to 180 degrees C. Oil an ovenproof lasagna dish (30 x 20 cm) Place a layer of vegetable on the bottom of the dish. Pour over 1/3 of the tomato sauce. Sprinkle basil and oregano over this layer.

Top with lasagna sheets. Spoon over 1/3 of the

white sauce. Smooth over the pasta. Repeat vegetable, tomato sauce, lasagna and white sauce layers until there are 3 layers of lasagna sheets. Spoon remaining white sauce over the top and spread out. Grate mozzarella over the top and scatter over the tomatoes. Bake for 40 - 45 minutes, uncovered until bubbling and cooked. Let sit for 15 minutes before cutting into serving squares.

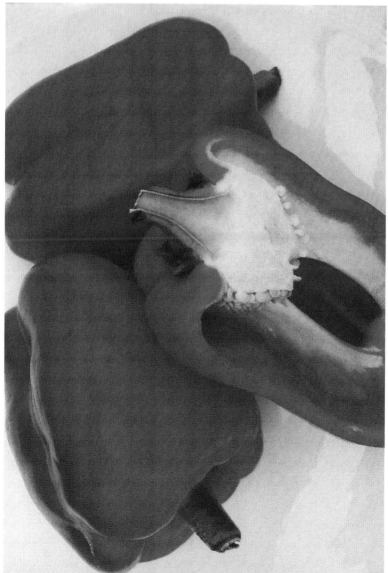

Roast Pumpkin and Spinach Lasagna

Serves: 6 - 8
Cooking time: 35 - 45 minutes

Ingredients

750g pumpkin or butternut

2 tbsp olive oil

1 sprig fresh rosemary

500g spinach, washed

freshly grated nutmeg

6 sheets lasagna

100g homemade mozzarella

Prepare pumpkin

Method

Pre-heat oven to 200 degrees C. Peel and deseed pumpkin or squash. Cut into 1 cm slices. Place on an oiled baking tray and season with black pepper. Place a sprig of rosemary on top. Roast until tender. Set aside.

Prepare spinach

Method

Cook spinach in saucepan with a little water on medium heat until the leaves wilt, about 5 minutes. Leave to cool. Squeeze water out. Place butter in a pan. Add spinach. Toss until spinach is coated in butter. Add pepper and grated nutmeg to season. Set aside.

For the white sauce

Ingredients

500ml milk
6 peppercorns
2 dried bay leaf
50g plain white flour
50g unsalted butter

Method

Place milk in saucepan with bay leaves and peppercorns. Then bring to boil and set aside to infuse. Remove bay leaf and peppercorns. Add flour and butter and whisk together until smooth. Heat gently until the sauce thickens. Remove from heat. Set aside.

For the tomato sauce

Ingredients

1 onion, chopped

1 tbsp olive oil

1 stalk celery, finely chopped

2 cloves garlic, finely chopped

400g can chopped Italian no salt tomatoes

1 tsp sugar

Method

Make the tomato sauce while pumpkin is roasting. Heat oil in a pan and add onion and garlic. Cook for 5 minutes until soft. Add celery and cook for 1 minute. Add tomatoes and sugar. Reduce heat and simmer uncovered for 30 minutes, stirring occasionally, until sauce thickens. Season with black pepper. Set aside.

For the lasagna

Heat oven to 200 degrees C. Grease a large lasagna dish or other ovenproof ceramic or glass dish of approximately 1.4 liter capacity. Place a layer of pumpkin in the bottom. Add a layer of spinach leaves. Then a layer of homemade tomato sauce. Place lasagna sheets on top. Add a layer of white sauce and a grating of cheese. Top with lasagna sheets, then pumpkin, spinach, tomato sauce, more lasagna and finally a layer of white sauce. Sprinkle remaining grated cheese on the top. Bake for 40 minutes or until the lasagna is golden and bubbling.

PIZZA

Rosemary Focaccia

Serves: 4 - 6
Cooking time: 40 minutes

Ingredients

1kg strong white bread flour

600ml warm water

3 x 7g sachets of dried yeast

1 tbsp white sugar

freshly ground black pepper

2 sprigs fresh rosemary

extra virgin olive oil

Method

Fill a small bowl with 3 tbsp warm water. Dissolve
in the sugar. Sprinkle yeast sachets on top and mix
well with a fork. Set aside for 10 minutes or until
frothy. Place flour in a large mixing bowl. Make a
well in the center. Add yeast mixture with the rest of
the water. Mix to make a soft dough.
Place dough on a dusted bench or wooden
board. Knead the dough, folding over, pushing

with the palms of your hands, folding over again and turning the dough for 5 minutes until the dough is elastic and smooth. Place dough in the bowl and cover with kitchen film and then a clean cloth. Place bowl in a warm place to rise, about 1 hour, until double in size. Remove cloth and kitchen film. Punch the dough down. Place on a lightly floured board and knead until smooth.

Grease a flat baking tray with oil. Dust with a little flour. Take the dough and flatten it onto the baking tray into a flat bread shape. Sprinkle rosemary leaves over the surface of the bread. Using your index finger, press to make indented dimples all over the surface. The dimples will help hold the olive oil while cooking. Drizzle dough with olive oil. Set the tray aside in a warm place for 1 hour until the bread has doubled in bulk.

Heat oven to 220 degrees C. Press your fingers over the dough to make indents for an authentic texture. Add freshly ground pepper.

Bake in a hot oven for 20 minutes, until golden brown and crusty. Remove from oven and tap the bottom of the bread, if it sounds hollow then it is cooked. Serve warm, dipped in extra virgin olive oil or topped with onion jam.

Napoletana Dough Recipe

Makes: 6 medium sized thin pizza bases

Ingredients

3 1/2 to 3 3/4 cups Italian Tipo '00' flour (or use strong white bread flour)

1 1/2 cups lukewarm water

1 1/2 tsp dry active yeast

1 tsp extra virgin olive oil

fine ground semolina for dusting the baking tray

Method

Place flour in a large mixing bowl. Make a well in the center. In a measuring jug, measure water and add dried yeast and sugar. Stir with a fork. Set aside for 5 minutes until frothy. Add the oil to this mixture. Pour into the well in the flour. Mix the liquid mixture into the flour. When the flour forms into a soft ball, place on a floured bench or wooden board. Knead for 5 minutes until the dough is smooth and elastic. Return to the bowl, cover with kitchen film and a clean cloth. Leave in a warm place for 1 hour until the dough is double in bulk. Punch down with your fist to push the air out. Shape into 6 balls. Roll out into circles and leave 15 minutes. Bake.

Pizza Sauce

This authentic recipe is for the oldest and most famous tomato sauce in Italian cooking.

Serves: 6
Cooking time: 30 minutes

Ingredients

400g can crushed Italian no low salt tomatoes

3 cloves garlic

6 tbsp olive oil

1/2 tsp coarsely ground black pepper

1/2 tsp sugar

fresh basil, large bunch, chopped finely

Method

Peel garlic cloves and chop medium to fine. Heat olive oil in a heavy bottomed pan and add garlic. Sauté until golden. Add tomatoes. Bring to boil, stirring constantly. Lower heat to medium. Add pepper and sugar. Stir well. Turn heat to low and simmer for 20 minutes until thick, stir at regular intervals. Remove from heat and add basil. Serve over pizza base.

Pizza Seafood Marinara

One of three traditional Neapolitan Pizzas.

Makes: 2 large pizzas
Cooking time: 30 minutes

Ingredients

2 cups chopped acid free tomatoes, no salt

5 tbsp garlic, chopped

3 tbsp extra virgin olive oil

2 tbsp fresh oregano leaves

1 cup seafood marinara mix

1 red pepper, cut in thin strips

freshly ground black pepper

Method

Roll out pizza dough (recipe above) into a circle. Place on a lightly greased baking tray dusted with finely ground semolina. Mix tomatoes with 3 tbsp oil and spread over rolled out pizza dough or use one cup tomato pizza/ pasta sauce from the Italian pantry in this book. Scatter with seafood mix and red pepper. Heat oven to 220 degrees C. Bake in hot oven 10 - 15 minutes.

Remove from oven and sprinkle with chopped garlic and oregano. Drizzle the olive oil over. Cook for 5 minutes more, taking care not to burn the garlic, to prevent garlic tasting bitter.

Pizza Margherita

Makes: 2 large pizzas
Cooking time: 30 minutes

Ingredients

3 tbsp extra virgin olive oil

1/2 cup tomato sauce (see recipe)

500g mozzarella cheese, low salt

20 fresh basil leaves

freshly ground black pepper

Method

Roll out pizza dough into two large 33cm rounds.
Brush each round with 1 tbsp olive oil. Divide the
tomato sauce in half and spread over each pizza
base. Sprinkle cheese on each pizza. Place basil
leaves on each pizza. Drizzle remaining olive oil
over pizzas and season with freshly ground black
pepper. Bake 20 - 30 minutes in a hot oven and
serve immediately.

Pizza Pugliese

A classic recipe from Pulgia in southern Italy uses potatoes for the pizza base.

Serves: 4
Cooking time: 30 minutes

Ingredients

225g potatoes
3/4 cup unbleached white flour
3 tbsp extra virgin olive oil
10 small tomatoes
1 tsp fresh oregano
freshly ground black pepper
200g low salt mozzarella cheese
bunch fresh basil, leaves removed, no stalks

Method

Boil potatoes. Cook until tender, about 30 minutes. Drain and pass through a sieve or ricer. Cool at room temperature. Do not refrigerate.
Mix potatoes with flour in a large bowl. Add a little water to help mixture form into a soft dough. Dust a board or bench lightly with flour. Place dough on

flour surface and roll out into a 30cm round. Grease a pizza-baking tray with oil. Place pizza on top. Drizzle oil over the top of the pizza. Add sliced tomatoes. Season with finely chopped oregano and freshly ground black pepper. Bake in a 200 degree C oven for 15 minutes. Remove from oven and top with mozzarella and fresh basil leaves. Bake 10 minutes longer until golden.

Shrimp Coriander Pizza

Makes: 2 pizzas
Cooking time: 30 minutes

Ingredients

500g fresh pizza dough

1 cup tomato pizza sauce

4 tbsp fresh coriander leaves

1 cup shrimp

1 cup mozzarella, cut into small chunks

1 red onion, finely sliced

olive oil infused with fresh basil or lemon

Method

Roll dough to make 2 pizza bases. Brush lightly with olive oil. Top with shrimp, red onion, mozzarella cheese, freshly ground black pepper, red chili flakes and a drizzle of olive oil. Cook at 220 C for 15 minutes or until crispy. Remove from oven and garnish with fresh coriander leaves.

Chicken Pizza

Makes: 4 pizzas
Cooking time: 30 minutes

Ingredients

1 kg pizza dough

11/2 cups tomato pizza sauce

1 large chicken breast, diced

1 cup pineapple diced, fresh or canned

100g unsalted cashew nuts

200g mascarpone cheese (or low salt cream
cheese) sesame seeds

coriander leaves, for garnish, oilve oil

Method

Divide pizza dough into 4. Roll out in circles to
make 4 pizza bases. Cook chicken breast in a little
olive oil, about 4 minutes. Remove from heat. Set
aside. Spoon tomato sauce over the bases. Spoon
chicken over and add cashews. Bake at 220 C
for 5 minutes. Remove and sprinkle cheese and
sesame seeds over and bake a further 10 minutes.
Remove from oven and top with coriander leaves.

Pizza Isolana

Makes: 2 pizzas
Cooking time: 25 minutes

Ingredients

500g fresh pizza dough

1 cup tomato pizza sauce

300g tuna (or use chicken breast)

1 avocado

1 cup mozzarella, cut in small cubes

2 tbsp chopped fresh aromatic herbs: lemongrass (white part only) and mint leaves. Or tarragon and thyme chopped together.

juice of 1 lemon or lime

flour

olive oil

black pepper, freshly ground

Method

Roll our pizza dough into 2 bases. Set aside. Mix 2 tbsp flour with your choice of herbs. Coat both sides of fish (or chicken). Heat 3 tbsp olive oil in a frying pan. Fry fish or chicken until golden brown on both sides. Remove and drain on kitchen paper. Slice the avocado and marinate 2 tsp of the lemon or lime juice. Spread tomato sauce over both bases. Drizzle with a little olive oil and a grind of black pepper. Slice chicken (or fish) into long strips. Place on the pizza in a wheel spoke pattern. Bake for 15 minutes in a 220 C oven. Remove from heat. Arrange avocado between chicken (or fish) slices, sprinkle cheese over. Bake for a further 5 minutes.

Lamb Sweet Potato Pizza

Serves: 4 - 5
Cooking time: 30 minutes

Ingredients

2 tbsp olive oil

1 sweet potato, peeled and thinly sliced

1 red onion, sliced

2 cloves garlic, finely chopped

1/2 tsp paprika

1 tsp ground fennel seeds

1/4 tsp dried red chili flakes

2 tsp ground coriander seeds

4 tbsp fresh coriander, chopped

black pepper, freshly ground

500g minced lamb

1/2 cup no salt pizza sauce

1/2 cup shredded low salt mozzarella cheese

1/4 cup flat-leaf parsley

Method:

Cook sweet potato and drain. Set aside. Heat olive oil in a large frying pan. Add onion and cook until golden and softened. Add paprika, chili flakes and coriander powder. Cook 1 minute. Add lamb. Cook for 5 minutes breaking it up with a spoon as you cook. Cook until most of the water has evaporated. Season with pepper and set aside. Prepare pizza bases by rolling out the dough into circles. Brush a little olive oil over the bases. Spoon tomato pizza sauce over the bases. Add lamb mixture, slices of sweet potatoes and cheese. Bake 15 minutes in a 220 C oven. Remove from heat and scatter coriander and parsley over before serving.

Pizza Toppings

By using the pizza dough, pizza sauce and mozzarella recipes (in this book), you can add any toppings you like to create your own signature pizzas. Here are more ideas.

Pizza with garlic and sausage

Use uncooked homemade sausage and finely chopped garlic. Spread tomato sauce over pizza base. Sprinkle with garlic and add crumbled sausage. Top with mozzarella. Drizzle with a few drops of olive oil, chopped oregano or basil. Bake.

Pizza with broccolini, tomatoes and sausage

Spoon 1/2 cup tomato pizza sauce over pizza base. Top with 1 1/2 cups mozzarella. Add 2 crumbled raw classic homemade Italian sausages. Bake until crisp. Top with sautéed broccolini and roasted cherry tomatoes. Sprinkle with oregano. Bake a further 5 minutes.

Pizza with mushroom

Spread tomato sauce on pizza base. Top with 1 cup of sliced mushrooms, 1/2 cup of homemade Italian sausage and some shredded mozzarella. Sprinkle with oregano leaves and a few drops of olive oil. Bake.

Pizza vegetarian

Cook vegetables first. Stewed or roasted peppers, eggplants, pumpkin, spinach, artichoke hearts, courgettes and what other vegetables you like. Spread tomato sauce over pizza base. Sprinkle with garlic, add cooked vegetables. Top with mozzarella. Drizzle a few drops of olive oil. Bake.

DESSERT

Sopranos Tiramisu

Tiramisu means "pick me up".

Serves: 12 large pieces - 16 small pieces
Cooking time: 30 minutes

Ingredients

4 eggs, separated

500g mascarpone cheese

200ml milk

4 - 5 tbsp sugar

3 tbsp amaretto liqueur

250g packet Savoiardi (lady fingers) boudoir
sponge biscuits.

2 tbsp unsweetened cocoa powder (sieved)

Method

Beat egg whites to form stiff peaks. Set aside.
In another bowl beat egg yolks until pale. Add
mascarpone cheese and mix until smooth. Fold in
egg whites. Mix milk and 2 tbsp amaretto, brandy,
frangelico or masala liqueur. Dip sponge fingers

into milk and liquor mixture. Place sponge fingers in a rectangular dish. Pour half the mascarpone mixture onto the biscuits. Add another layer of soaked biscuits. Pour the rest of the mascarpone over the top. Place covered in the fridge overnight. Dust with cocoa powder before serving.

Eggless Easy Tiramisu

Ingredients

3/4 cup heavy cream

1 cup mascarpone cheese

2 tsp vanilla extract

3 tbsp marsala wine, to taste

6 tbsp icing sugar (powdered sugar)

1 cup milk

26 - 30 savoiardi biscuits (sponge fingers)

chocolate, shaved

unsweetened cocoa for decoration

Method

Whip cream with 4 tbsp sugar until soft stiff peaks. Set aside. Mix mascarpone cheese with vanilla essence and masala wine. Fold mascarpone mixture into the cream. Combine milk with 2 tbsp icing sugar with a little masala wine, to taste. Dip biscuits into the milk mixture. Place in a rectangular dish. Spread a layer of masala cream over the sponge fingers. Sprinkle with chocolate shavings.

Cover with a layer of sponge fingers. Repeat layers until the sponge fingers and cream mixture are used up, finishing with a cream layer. Dust this layer with powdered cocoa. Cover and place in the fridge a few hours before serving. Or overnight.

Ricotta
with Honey

A classic dessert using homemade ricotta. Serve with stewed or poached berries or stewed stone fruit, or on its own.

Serves: 4
Cooking time: 10 minutes

Ingredients

400g fresh ricotta
50g vanilla sugar
100ml pure liquid honey

Method

Heat oven to 200 C
Place ricotta in 4 small baking dishes. Mix lemon zest with sugar and sprinkle over the ricotta. Cook for 5 - 7 minutes. Remove from oven and drizzle with a little honey. Serve with warm poached or stewed fruit.

Pistachio Biscotti

Makes: 36 biscotti

Ingredients

3 cups unsalted whole almonds

3/4 cup granulated sugar

2 tsp baking powder

1 tsp almond essence

2 1/2 cups plain flour

4 large eggs, plus one egg for brushing tops

Method

Heat oven to 180 degrees C. Line a baking sheet with baking paper. Place almonds on the sheet and toast for 10 minutes in the oven. Remove from oven. In a large mixing bowl mix sugar, baking powder, flour and almonds together using a large spoon. In a medium bowl whisk eggs with almond essence until blended together. Add this to the flour mixture. Dust hands and mix until a soft dough forms. Divide the dough into 4 balls. Flour a work surface and roll out each ball into a log shape.

Dust hands with flour to work with the dough.

Repeat making all the dough into log shapes.

Place 2 logs on each baking sheet. Brush logs with beaten egg. Bake in oven for 30 - 40 minutes. Leave to cool for 10 minutes.

Slice each log diagonally using a serrated knife. Cut each log into 10 pieces. Place cookies flat side down on the baking tray. Turn off oven. Place the cookies into the oven to dry out for 30 minutes. You can leave them longer, up to 60 minutes, if you want to create hard biscotti. Remove from oven. You can store biscotti in an airtight container or tin for up to 1 month.

Anise and Orange Biscotti

Makes about: 20 biscotti

Ingredients

1 cup unsalted pine nuts

3/4 cup granulated sugar

2 tsp baking powder

2 cups plain flour

3 large eggs,

1 egg lightly beaten, for brushing tops

1 tbsp anise seeds, crushed

1 tsp vanilla essence

1 tbsp finely grated orange zest

Method

Heat oven to 180 degrees C. Line a baking sheet with baking paper. Place pine nuts on the sheet and toast for 5 minutes until golden. Remove from oven. Place pine nuts, sugar, baking powder and flour in a mixing bowl. Whisk eggs. Crush anise seeds using a spice mill or mortar and pestle. Place seeds in a frying pan and toast for 3 minutes taking care not to burn. Add the seeds, vanilla and orange zest to the whisked eggs. Mix to make a sticky dough. Dust hands and mix until a soft dough forms. Divide the dough into 4 balls.

Flour a work surface and roll out each ball into a log shape. Dust hands with flour to work with the dough. Repeat making all the dough into log shapes. Place 2 logs on each baking sheet. Brush logs with beaten egg. Bake trays in oven for 30 - 40 minutes, turning the trays so the logs are golden. Leave to cool for 10 minutes.

Slice each log diagonally using a serrated knife. Cut each log into 10 pieces. Place cookies flat side down on the baking tray. Be sure to turn off the oven first. Then place the cookies into the oven to dry for 30 minutes. You can leave them longer, up to 60 minutes, if you want to create hard biscotti. Remove from oven and cool on a wire rack. When completely cool, you can store biscotti in an airtight container for up to 1 month.

Zabaglione

Serves: 4
Cooking time: 20 minutes

Ingredients

5 large eggs yolks
1/3 cup sugar
1/3 cup marsala wine
blackberries, blueberries, strawberries

Method

Place egg yolks, sugar and wine in a bowl and whisk together. Whip together until well blended. Place bowl over a pot of simmering water on medium heat. Whisk over simmer water until thick and foamy. Cool and serve with fresh berries.

Balsamic Strawberries

Serves: 4 - 6
Cooking time: 5 minutes

Ingredients

1 punnet fresh strawberries, quartered

2 1/2 tbsp balsamic vinegar

1 tbsp sugar

1/4 tsp freshly ground black pepper

freshly grated lemon zest

Method

Combine strawberries, balsamic, sugar and pepper in a serving bowl. Leave for 30 minutes to 1 hour at room temperature before serving.

Dust with lemon zest and serve.

Strawberries and Blueberries

Serves: 4

Ingredients

1 punnet of fresh strawberries

1 cup seedless green grapes

1 cup blueberries (or raspberries)

1 tbsp sugar

2 tsp fresh mint

Method

Wash fruit, hull and quarter. Combine with sugar in a bowl. Cover for 1 hour. Serve chilled.

Amaretto Stuffed Peaches

Serves: 4
Cooking time: 25 minutes

Ingredients

4 peaches

2 tbsp unsalted softened butter

3 tbsp brown sugar

1/2 cup ground almonds (or 6 crushed amaretto cookies)

masala wine or amaretto liqueur

Method

Preheat oven to 160 degrees C. Wash and halve the peaches. Remove stones. Place cut side up in a baking dish. Mix butter, sugar and ground almonds together. You can add a few drops of almond essence, chopped dried cherries, or chopped crystalized ginger to this mixture.
Add a spoonful to each peach. Drizzle with liqueur. Place 3 tbsp of water in the bottom of the dish. Bake uncovered for 20 minutes until the topping is

golden brown. Top with juice from the pan. Serve with a little cream or mascarpone.

Note: you can use hazelnuts, pecans, or walnuts. You can also use nectarines instead of peaches.

Italian Lemon Ice

Serves: 4 - 6

Ingredients

2 cups warm water
1/2 cup sugar
1/2 cup lemon juice

Method

Dissolve sugar in water in a small saucepan.
Add lemon juice. Pour into freezing tray and freeze.
Remove from freezer and stir frequently . Return
to freezer. Repeat until thick and mushy. Serve
garnished with mint leaves.

Vanilla Bean Panna Cotta

Panna cotta means 'cooked cream'.

Serves: 6 - 8
Cooking time: 30 minutes

Ingredients

2 cups milk

1 envelope of unflavored gelatin (2 tsp)

1/2 cup plain yogurt

1 vanilla pod

1/3 cup sugar

1/2 cup whipping cream

Method

Place milk in a saucepan with split vanilla pod. Heat milk and vanilla on medium heat for 5 minutes. Take care not to boil. Remove vanilla pod and scrape seeds. Return seeds to the milk and discard the pod.

Place 1/4 cup milk in a bowl and sprinkle gelatin on surface. Stir. Stand for 5 minutes. Set bowl of gelatin in simmering water and stir until gelatin is dissolved. Add sugar and stir until sugar is dissolved. Remove from heat. Place remaining milk in a bowl with yogurt and vanilla seeds.

Slowly whisk gelatin mixture into the milk mixture. Place bowl in the fridge for 30 minutes or until it starts to thicken.

Beat cream in an electric mixer until soft peaks form. Whisk into the milk and yogurt mixture until smooth. Spoon mixture into 1/2 cup size china or glass custard cups. Cover and place in the fridge for 4 hours or up to two days.

To serve, run a knife around the sides to loosen the panna cotta. Invert onto a serving plate. Serve with fresh fruit or biscotti biscuits.

Sicilian Ricotta Cassata Cake

Ingredients

1 cup homemade ricotta cheese

1/4 cup icing sugar (confectioners sugar)

3 tbsp semisweet chocolate, finely chopped

3 tbsp Italian glacé fruits, chopped

3 1/2 tsp amaretto liqueur

2 tbsp water

1 tsp grated orange zest

24 ladyfinger biscuits

Method

Place ricotta cheese, icing sugar and 2 tbsp of chocolate, orange zest, glacé fruits and amaretto into a bowl and whisk together.

Mix remaining amaretto with water in a small bowl. Dip sponge fingers into amaretto to flavor them. Then place 6 fingers on a serving dish. Spread with 1/3 ricotta cheese mixture. Add another 6 sponge fingers on top. Place another 1/3 of the ricotta mixture on top. Repeat layering, finishing with sponge fingers. Dust with a little icing sugar, sprinkle with remaining chocolate. Cover with kitchen plastic wrap and place in the fridge for 4 hours or overnight before cutting into serving pieces.

Fresh Summer Fruitcake

Makes: 1 large cake

Ingredients

1 cup unblanched almonds
1/2 cup sugar
1/3 cup flour
2 eggs
1/2 cup milk
4 tbsp unsalted butter, melted
900g sweet ripe apricots, pitted and sliced

Method

Heat over to 180 degrees C.

Butter a 25cm springform pan. Place almonds and sugar in a blender or food processor and pulse in slow bursts until finely ground. Add flour. Pulse on slow. Place into a mixing bowl. Set aside.

In a medium mixing bowl place eggs, milk and melted butter. Mix well together. Add the egg mixture into the flour mixture. Beat until the batter is smooth. Pour into baking tin. Smooth the surface.

Place apricots on top.

Bake for 40 minutes or until a skewer inserted into the center comes out clean. Cool on a wire rack.

Note: You can use other fruit such as plums, peaches, nectarines or fresh berries. Strawberries, blueberries or raspberries. You can vary the nutmeal. Use walnuts, hazelnuts or pecans.

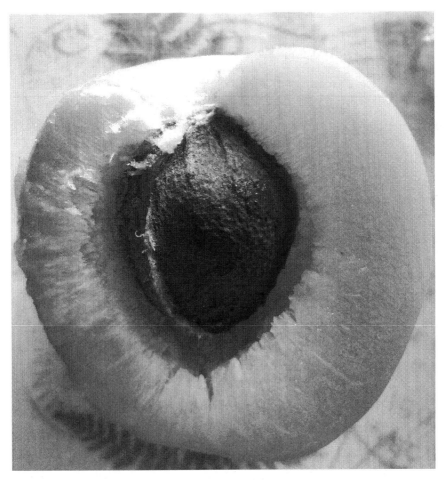

Strawberry Mousse

Serves: 6 - 8
Cooking time: 30 minutes

Ingredients

1/3 cup sugar

1/4 cup water

2 envelopes unflavored gelatin

1/2 tsp pure almond extract

450g strawberries, washed and hulled

1 1/2 cups homemade ricotta

Method

Place water and sugar in a small saucepan and
mix until combined over low heat.
Remove from heat. Sprinkle gelatin over the
surface to soften. Set aside. Place strawberries
in a food processor or blender and puree. Add
softened gelatin mixture, ricotta and almond
extract. Blend. Place mixture into serving bowls.
Place covered in fridge for 6 - 8 hours or overnight.
Note: You can use other summer berries or

fresh fruit in this recipe such as raspberries, boysenberries, blueberries or use stone fruit such as peaches or apricots.

M E A S U R E M E N T S

Oven temperatures

Degree F		Degree C
200	=	100
225	=	110
250	=	120
275	=	140
300	=	150
325	=	160
350	=	180
375	=	190
400	=	200
425	=	220
450	=	230
475	=	240

Liquid Measures

1 tsp	=	5 mls
1 tbsb	=	20 mls
4 cups	=	1 liter
1/2 cup	=	125 mls

Solid measures

32 oz	=	1 kilogram
16 oz	=	500 grams
8oz	=	250 grams
7oz	=	220 grams
6 oz	=	185 grams
5 oz	=	155 grams
4 oz	=	125 grams
3 oz	=	90 grams
2 oz	=	60 grams
1 oz	=	30 grams

Meniere Man
Books

Let's Get Better
A Memoir of Meniere's Disease

**From Meniere sufferer to Meniere survivor.
A truly remarkable and successful recovery story without surgery.**

Let's Get Better CD
Relaxing & Healing Guided Meditation

Personally guided meditation, created especially for Meniere sufferers. Helps relieve stress and anxiety. Promotes healing and renewed energy.

Vertigo Vertigo
About Vertigo About Dizziness and What You Can Do About it.

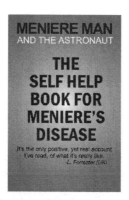

Meniere Man And The Astronaut
The Self Help Book for Meniere's Disease
Voted by Goodreads as 'A Book Everyone Should Read at Least Once in Their Lifetime'

Meniere Man And The Butterfly.
The Meniere Effect
How to Minimize the Effect of Meniere's on Family,
Money, Lifestyle, Dreams and You.

Meniere Man In The Kitchen.
Recipes That Helped Me Get Over Meniere's
Delicious nutritious low salt recipes from our family
kitchen.

Meniere Man and the Film Director.
The Self Help Book for Meniere's Attacks.
Shows you exactly how to cope before during and after a vertigo attack. Real practical, helpful advice you can use to help with vertigo attacks.

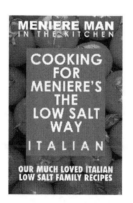

Meniere Man In The Kitchen.
Cooking For Meniere's
The Low Salt Way.
Italian.

**Meniere Man In The Himalayas.
Low Salt Curries**

About The Author

At the height of his business career and aged just forty-six, he suddenly became acutely ill. He was diagnosed with Meniere's disease, but the full impact of having Meniere's disease was to come later. He was to lose not only his health, but his career and financial status as he knew it. He began to lose all hope that he would fully recover a sense of well-being. But it was his personal spirit and desire to get 'back to normal' that made him not give up to a life of Meniere's symptoms of severe vertigo, dizziness and nausea.

He decided that you can't put a limit on anything in life. Rather than letting Meniere's disease get in the way of recovery, he started to focus on what to do about overcoming Meniere's disease.

These days life is different for the Author. He is a fit

active man who has no symptoms of Meniere's disease except for hearing loss and tinnitus in one ear. Following his own advice he continues to avoid salt, stress, takes vitamins, exercises regularly and maintains a positive, mindful attitude. He does not take any medication.

All the physical activities he enjoys these days require a high degree of balance and equilibrium: snowboarding, surfing, hiking, windsurfing, weightlifting, and riding a motorbike.

Meniere Man believes that if you want to experience a marked improvement in health you can't wait until you feel well to start. You must begin to improve your health now, even though you don't feel like it.

The Author is a writer, painter, designer and artist. He is married to a poet. They have two adult children. He spends most days writing or painting. He enjoys the sea, cooking, travel, photography, nature and the great company of family, friends and his beloved dog, Bella.

Additional Information

If you enjoyed this Meniere Man book and you think it could be helpful to others, please leave a review for the book on amazon.com, amazon.co.uk or Goodreads. Thank you for your support.

Meniere Support Networks

Meniere's Society (UNITED KINGDOM)
www. menieres.org.uk
Meniere's Society Australia (AUSTRALIA)
info@menieres.org.au
The Meniere's Resource & Information Centre (AUSTRALIA)
www.menieres.org.au
Healthy Hearing & Balance Care (AUSTRALIA)
www.healthyhearing.com.au
Vestibular Disorders association (AUSTRALIA)
www.vestibular .org
The Dizziness and Balance Disorders Centre (AUSTRALIA)
www.dizzinessbalancedisorders.com
Meniere's Research Fund Inc   (AUSTRALIA)
www.menieresresearch.org.au
Australian Psychological Society APS (AUSTRALIA)
www.psychology.org.au
Meniere's Disease Information Center (USA)
www.menieresinfo.com
Vestibular Disorders Association (USA)
www.vestibular.org
BC Balance and Dizziness Disorders Society (CANADA)
www.balanceand dizziness.org
Hearwell (NEW ZEALAND)
www.hearwell.co.nz
WebMD.
www.webmd.com
National Institute for Health
www.medlineplus.gov
Mindful Living Program
www.mindfullivingprograms.com
Center for Mindfulness
www. umassmed.edu.com

Made in the USA
Middletown, DE
07 January 2018